S0-BFF-695

EQUAL MARRIAGE

JEAN STAPLETON

EQUAL MARRIAGE

RICHARD BRIGHT

ABINGDON NASHVILLE

Equal Marriage

Library of Congress Cataloging in Publication Data

STAPLETON, JEAN, 1942-
Equal marriage.
Bibliography: p.
1. Marriage. 2. Equality. 3. Intimacy (Psychology) 4. Social role. I. Bright, Richard, 1931- joint author. II. Title.
HQ734.S847 301.42'7 76-19048

ISBN 0-687-11993-6

Manufactured by the Parthenon Press at
Nashville, Tennessee, United States of America

DEDICATION

To the memory of our first spouses, John F. Clegg and Flora Stryker Bright, who contributed greatly and lovingly to our understanding of marriage as an equal partnership and with whom we groped toward equality—without any knowledge of where we were going, without a woman's movement, and without any book on equal marriage.

PREFACE

Anyone learning something new seeks guidance from friends, family, teachers, and books, especially if that something new is as important as how to be married.

When each of us was newly married the first time, our acquaintances made the assumption that wives would play certain roles and husbands would play certain other roles. Though each could help the other, the assumption remained that the roles were basic to a normal life.

When we reached for books on marriage, hoping they could help us develop marriages more suited to our personalities, we were either prompted to accept the rigid roles or given sound advice—but with examples that still put men and women in rigid roles. Both of us finally decided we did not want to live the traditional life, and so we struck out on our own to develop a new kind of marriage, a marriage of equals.

In the last decade we have been waiting for a book that would address itself to our kind of marriage and how to have one, but we haven't found such a book. We had hopes when we saw titles such as *Open Marriage* and *Liberated Marriage,* but we were disappointed to find that they were either basic books on women's liberation, anti-marriage, or against intimacy in marriage. This book is none of these. It consists of how to live as equals in a marriage and reap the reward of not only having greater personal fulfillment but also of having a better marriage.

Richard Bright is a marriage, family, and child counselor in California. He previously spent twenty years in campus ministry. He was married thirteen years to Flora Stryker Bright, with whom he had two children. They were working toward an equal marriage when she died in 1971.

Jean Stapleton is head of the Journalism Department at East Los Angeles College and previously was a reporter with a wire service and several newspapers. She had an equal marriage with John Clegg for seven years until he died in 1972.

We married each other in 1973. Establishing a second equal marriage was easier for us than it had been the first time because we could use what we had learned before as a guide.

As a marriage counselor, Richard has found that there is no such thing as an intimate marriage that is not an equal marriage.

And a marriage that is not intimate may lack conflict, but it will never have the deep satisfaction of an intimate marriage. Without intimacy, partners remain lonely even though they are part of a couple.

We are both very active in the National Organization for Women, and, as feminists, we believe that equal marriage is the only kind of marriage that does not deny the personhood of either partner.

PREFACE

This book is about how couples in equal marriages have worked out their equality in every aspect of marriage from chores to sex to child-rearing.

It is possible to have an equal, intimate marriage from the very beginning. By establishing your ground rules in advance and being committed to the concept of equality, you can start marriage as best friends and remain best friends to the end.

Or, if you have gotten off to an unequal start, you can change and become equals; you can reestablish your friendship.

When we were first learning how to have an equal marriage, we didn't have any guideposts. We didn't even know if it were possible to have equality in marriage.

Now we know it is possible to have equal marriage. This book can give you some guideposts so you can more quickly and smoothly achieve the goal of equality than those of us who headed blindly toward that goal in the days before the woman's movement.

CONTENTS

CHAPTER 1
WHAT IS EQUAL MARRIAGE?

Using the words *equal* and *marriage* in the same phrase may seem a contradiction of terms to many people. It is often said that in any relationship one person must be dominant—that people, like chickens, must have a pecking order.

To anyone who accepts that idea, it must seem impossible for a marriage to exist in which the partners are equal and no one is dominant. But human beings are more complex and far more intelligent than chickens. People have the power to determine for themselves what type of relationship they will have and to change customs that are no longer functional.

Equal marriage means having the same status in the relationship, the same responsibility for success of the relationship, and the same responsibility for the couple's survival in the world. It does not mean looking alike or having the same talents and skills or liking the same things or making the same amount of money. An equal relationship is too complicated for a chicken but not for an adult human being. In fact, we believe that all good marriages—creative, emotionally satisfying ones—are equal marriages.

You are probably busy thinking of exceptions to that. But think carefully about the relationship. Often people use the language of unequal relationships to describe their own marriages, even in the case of equal marriage, just because those are the words they have always heard used to describe marriage. One of our own relatives told us her husband was the "head of the family." We asked what that meant to her. "If I want to take a trip and he doesn't feel like it, we don't go," she said. We asked what happened if he wanted to take a trip and she didn't feel like it. "We don't go," she answered.

In other words, these two persons have a great deal of respect for each other and do not force each other to travel against either's will; they each have an equal say in their travel plans. They share many other decisions about their life together. However, they grew up accepting terms like "head of the household," and anyone who heard them discussing their marriage might think the husband was a patriarch ruling his household with a heavy hand instead of being the equal partner he is.

Equal marriage is two whole persons coming together. In the past, marriage has been two half-persons coming together to make one viable unit. Children were taught to expect to find a spouse to make up for all their deficiencies so that the "two become one," a complete whole.

For that reason, girls were trained from birth in

housekeeping, cooking, and child-rearing. They were rewarded for quietness, patience, and good needlework. They were allowed to laugh generously and cry freely when physically or emotionally hurt, but they were taught to suppress anger. They soon learned that the only right answer to the question "What are you going to be when you grow up?" was "a mommy." They were given toys to act as props for family dramas and discouraged from athletic or mechanical toys. They were told that "girls are good in English," and so they applied themselves to that field while dodging math. And they learned not to worry their "pretty little heads" about such weighty matters as understanding insurance, filling out income tax forms, buying property, managing money, and knowing other things necessary for survival in our society because someday a man will come along, "and he'll be big and strong" and knowledgeable about such things and take care of her, and she'll live happily ever after. And so, if she were a very good little girl, she would do as she was taught and apply herself to learning to care for house, husband, and children, while ignoring her intellectual development and avoiding any salable job skills with which she could earn her own living.

Which is not to say that little boys were much better off. They were trained to be half-persons too, but they were the other half, the half that couldn't take care of itself but could support the family. They were rewarded for being tough and for hiding their pain when hurt emotionally or physically. They learned that boisterous, aggressive behavior proved they were "all boy." They found that grown-ups really wanted them to have some idea when they asked "What do you want to be when you grow up?" and it had better be a he-man profession, not just "a daddy" or "a husband" and certainly nothing girlish like "a teacher." They were allowed to express anger freely but not tenderness. They were given action toys—sports equipment, transportation toys, and mechanical toys which taught the use of their bodies, but not much about human relations. They learned that English is "sissy," but "boys are good at math," so they applied themselves to numbers, expecting to succeed. If they tried to learn to cook their meals or sew their own rips, they were teased. No one trusted them with young children, but they had to find other ways to make money besides baby-sitting because from their first date they knew that the financial burden of women and children would always be theirs.

Together, these two half-persons could make it. They could earn a living and spend it and feed and clothe themselves and care for their children and handle their income tax and laugh and cry and be angry and fix the lawn mower and talk to the mechanic and write letters.

But apart they were lost, so they knew they must cling together no matter how bad the relationship. Many of these relationships still exist, and they come to marriage counselors hoping to patch up a poor relationship and stay afloat.

Even more commonly, a woman will want out of such a marriage but will cling to it knowing that she cannot survive without her husband's economic support, and so she becomes a "kept" woman rather than a partner.

Or, a man wants out of the marriage, but he knows he must continue to support his estranged wife and children, and he knows he must then have another wife in order to survive and that he cannot support two families. So he, too, feels trapped in the marriage.

Men and women who were raised to have only half the skills required for living and to exhibit only half the traits of a full human being will equal together in marriage only one person.

Equal marriage partners have not necessarily been raised differently. But, wanting to be whole persons or knowing they do not want to cling to a marriage that is bankrupt purely for survival, they learn the skills they need to survive in this world, and they learn together to exhibit freely the traits that were once considered the exclusive characteristics of the other sex.

Being capable of living alone creatively, equal marriage partners choose to be together. They do not have to be together. Being whole, they know they can live without each other if necessary, so they don't have to hold on so desperately that they crush each other as half-persons often do.

More than anything else, equal marriage is an attitude—one of mutual respect. An equal partner doesn't devalue what the other partner thinks is important. Such a partner doesn't consider her or his work more valuable than the spouse's or expect special privileges. Equal marriage is loving and honoring your spouse as much as you love and honor yourself—and if you don't love and honor yourself, you'll make a poor partner.

Two persons who have that kind of respect for each other can be open with each other, and so equal marriage is free of games. It means asking for what you want, knowing your spouse wants you to have what you want if it is possible, instead of trying to trick your spouse into giving you what you want.

On the other hand, when one partner is dominant and the other partner is in a one-down position, game-playing is almost automatic. Traditionally the wife has been the powerless one, the one in the one-down position. The one-down person cannot make decisions or take action and so must act through the spouse. Women in the one-down position are almost powerless to avoid being bitchy, nagging, and/or conniving, and those are terms we hear used to stereotype wives. Being powerless to get what they want for themselves, they must try to force or trick their men into giving them what they want. Interestingly, many marriages exist in which the man takes the one-down position, and his behavior could be described in the same way. Passive-aggressive behavior, as such behavior is called, is not so much a trait of personality as it is a product of the one-down position.

A marriage with that type of structure is uncomfortable for both partners. It is unpleasant to be nagged, berated, and tricked. It is equally unpleasant to feel powerless and so unhappy that you feel compelled to behave that way. And yet, most people accept the one-up–one-down structure as basic to marriage.

Many people are groping for a better kind of marriage. Some have found equal marriage on their own. Some women have taken courses in "superfemininity" and believe they have found the answer. Others swear by the book *Open Marriage* as a solution. Equal marriage is a solution between these extremes.

The courses spawned by the books *Total Woman* and *Fascinating Womanhood* do work; that is, they create a marriage in which the lines of power and the duties are clear, so they reduce the conflict. The woman is encouraged to act as childlike as possible, leaving the breadwinning and decision-making to the man and, emotionally, intellectually, and even physically, imitating a little girl. That forces her husband to become her daddy/ruler—a simple, conflict-free relationship, unless his decisions cause her to suffer. In that case, resentment is bound to build up and come out as, yes, nagging, bitchiness, or trickery. Trickery is the method encouraged by such courses which not only perpetuate game-playing but also give helpful hints about how to win the games. Such a marriage can be peaceful. It can never be intimate or creative.

Open Marriage goes to the other extreme. It features many of the characteristics of equal marriage: mutual respect, growth, absence of game-playing, lack of forced sex roles. It differs from equal marriage in that it lacks commitment and intimacy. That may seem minor, but, as far as we are concerned, there is no reason for marriage if you lack the commitment that makes intimacy possible.

Marriage has been called a dying institution. Some

experts have predicted that it will vanish altogether and will be replaced by couples' living together with no legal recognition, no vows of fidelity, no long-term commitment. We do not believe it will happen.

Loveless marriages may die out, and they should. Neurotic, game-playing marriages may die out and should. Marriage for money or status may die out and should. Marriage as a device for allowing half-persons to survive may die out and should. Marriage for sex alone is already nearly dead. Intimate, game-free marriages will thrive because there is no substitute for them. Intimacy only thrives when the commitment is unconditional and long-range, as in marriage, and intimacy is only possible when two persons are equals.

Marriage is not a dying institution. It is a changing one. Today more people marry at some time in their lives than ever before. Today more people divorce than ever before, too, not just because divorce is easier now but because they expect much more of a marriage.

A growing number of women are refusing to participate in a relationship in which they are not equal. A growing number of men are finding that an equal relationship is so rewarding that they are not interested in any other kind.

That means that marriages of the future will be commitments of two equals to each other, that intimacy will be increasingly the goal toward which couples strive in their marriages. It does not mean divorce will lessen, necessarily, because people will not want to settle for a relationship that does not achieve intimacy.

Although marriage began as an economic and sometimes political institution, it will not continue as such. Fully independent human beings will have the freedom to choose marriage for intimacy. It isn't common, but some equal-partnership marriages have already achieved game-free intimacy. Someday it will be the one-up–one-down relationship which will be strange.

CHAPTER 2
WHAT'S IN IT FOR YOU?

Nobody gets married just so they can be lonely; yet millions of married people find they *are* lonely. They start out loving each other so much that they can't bear to be apart and thinking that marriage or living together will make them closer. It could, but too often their idea of marriage pulls them apart. He is pushed out into the "man's world" of work, and she is left with the "woman's world" of home and children. As each tries to live up to the role expectations for that sex, the couple is polarized and tends to have less and less in common. Not understanding each other, they easily fall into blaming each other. "You and me against the world" becomes you and me against each other.

By ending their artificial separation of tasks, of goals, of emotions, both men and women stand to gain much in companionship and intimacy.

Both sexes also stand to gain much by being freed of some of their traditional role expectations, although both also stand to lose some privileges in order to gain the greater benefits of equality.

At first glance, equal marriage may seem to be an especially bad deal for men. After thousands of years as head of the household, men may fear that equal marriage is an attempt to pull them down to women's traditional subservient level and elevate women to head of the household in their place.

To make marriage equal is not to reverse the roles. It is to develop a new kind of marriage, one in which no one is the *head* of the household, and new ways of relating to each other must be learned.

To be honest, men do lose a few privileges when they become partners in marriage instead of boss of the family, though many of these "privileges" aren't as valuable as they might once have seemed.

What does a man have to lose?

1. If you are the kind of man who expects to come home every evening to a meal cooked by your wife and a house cleaned by her, no matter how busy she may be with her job or other activities, then you will find you must share the responsibilities of preparing the meals and cleaning the house.

2. If you are the kind of father who expects to have the children kept out of your way when you come home from work until you rest and then play with them a short time until your wife puts them to bed, you will find yourself much more involved in child care.

3. If you have expected to have the last say on family finances, choice of where to live and in what style, or how the family spends its leisure time, you will find that you will *share* those decisions.

4. If you believe a man must be tough, decisive, unemotional, aloof from domestic affairs, and always

right in his decisions, you will be changing your concept of masculinity.

5. If you have always considered it your prerogative to spend most evenings and weekends on yourself, watching football or reading or pursuing a hobby, you will find that you spend more of your time sharing household and child-rearing chores. And your wife will have a bit more free time, which she may want to spend with you.

6. If you are the kind of man who expects many personal favors from your wife as a matter of course, you will have to stop thinking of her as your personal servant. She will no longer shuffle off to the kitchen obediently if you yell orders at her like Archie Bunker's "Bring me a beer, Edith."

7. If you are confident that you know exactly how life should be and have been living as though your marriage were a script handed to you by your parents or your peer group, you will lose the security of living predictably. In an equal marriage, you don't know how to behave in every situation, and you have to work out situations with logic or by trying different behaviors until you find one that is comfortable.

Interestingly, most of these "losses" are just the reverse side of what men have to gain from equal marriage:

1. In sharing the household and child-care tasks, you become a real partner to your wife, and you will have a better relationship. Two equals may share their lives, thoughts, and emotions freely. In contrast, an authoritarian husband would have to hide any anxiety or indecisiveness, while a subordinate wife would

have to hide any activities and thoughts she thought the "boss" would not approve.

2. In sharing child care, you develop a real relationship with your children, one in which the children are not trying to impress Father or evade his punishment but one in which they know him as a person and feel comfortable confiding in him. Such a father will have real influence in guiding his children through the experiences of childhood and adolescence.

3. Just as you will be sharing more of the burdens of housekeeping and child-rearing, your wife will be able to share the burden of earning a living, taking the pressure off you. Whether and how much she works is an individual couple's decision, just as it is the couple's decision whether the husband will work and how much. They may decide to live on her income while he goes back to school, or her part-time work may free him from having to moonlight to make ends meet. Having an earning wife will relieve your fear of losing your job, as well as the pressure to keep a job you loathe but keep just for the steady income. Unless you are in a very high tax bracket, having two incomes is bound to make life more comfortable. In fact, the government reports that many of the families earning more than $10,000 a year do so only because both spouses work.

4. If you stop defining masculinity in the traditional way, you will be free to do things once considered feminine without feeling threatened. Many men enjoy cooking and child care; football star Rosey Grier has even had the courage to take up needlepoint. None of

the men reports any ill effects. Under the old definition of masculinity, men would have to forgo such enjoyable activities, at great loss to themselves. You will also be free to admit to not knowing everything, to not being sure about every decision, and you will be able to express emotions other than anger and pride. Likewise, you may be surprised to find your wife learning to do things once considered masculine, such as household repairs and understanding the stock market, and not being any less sexy for her new abilities.

5. You will discover that being born male and growing up makes you a man. You won't have to waste your life proving your manhood by conquering women or performing acts of bravado or drinking too much or being violent, ways that many men, such as the late Ernest Hemingway, have used to convince themselves that they really are men.

6. You may gain the companionship of your wife for those interests you have in common, now that you are sharing the chores and she has a little more free time. You may discover that she loves football, too, or that your fishing trips can be combined with her rock-hounding.

7. You won't have to feel guilty about your wife's giving up a promising career for you. If she gives it up it will be because she wanted to or she was not as successful as she expected to be; if she decides to pursue it, both the decision and the success will have been hers, but you can have the same pride in her work as she has in yours.

8. You will gain an interesting companion (or keep

one) as your wife takes on outside interests and grows as a person. You won't find yourselves, as so many married couples do, sitting across the table from each other at a restaurant and looking bored because you have nothing to say to each other. The conversation and the companionship will remain lively, something you'll remain eager to return to each day.

Some men will probably think that they have a right to feel superior to their wives because the wife *is* inferior. Psychological studies have shown that to be a rarity. A couple may not be equal in intelligence, but the less intelligent person may have more social ability or more creativity. The couple may not be equally attractive, but the less attractive person will have money or a prized quality to make up for it.

If you feel your wife is no longer your equal, perhaps you should look into why that is so. While you have been out in the world learning a job and meeting new people, has she been taking care of small children with no relief and no adults to talk with? Have you had time for reading while she was washing dishes? A more equal marriage could make your wife a more equal person.

Women, too, have a few things to lose in having an equal marriage though, again, these seem less like "privileges" when they are looked at more closely.

1. If you are the kind of woman who looks upon your husband as a meal ticket, a provider of goodies, you will have to realize that you too are capable of providing. You may need to go back to school or update your skills in order to be employable. But you will have to realize that your husband may not always

be there, that he may need or want a chance to go back to school or stay out of work for a while for some other reason, that he could be incapacitated, or that you may be able to make the difference between just getting by and being comfortable, and that the whole family is suffering by your not taking a job.

2. If you like the feeling of being the hub of the family, the "queen mother," you will have to be ready to share that central position with your husband as he develops close relationships with the children and shares in their care.

3. If you have enjoyed the position of having your husband make all the decisions while you blame him for anything that goes wrong, you will have to get used to sharing the responsibility for your joint decisions.

4. If you are used to winning arguments or getting your way by being emotional, you will have to start being straight about saying what you want and be prepared to give good reasons for it without getting overemotional.

5. If you usually get your husband or some other man to do all the heavy, dirty, or mechanical work on the grounds that you are too weak, dainty, and incompetent to do it because you are a woman, you may have to learn to carry your share of the load to the limit of your physical ability.

6. If you want to be placed on a pedestal and looked up to simply because you are a woman, you'll have to get used to being treated as a person and not having the one-up position occasionally as a compensation for your usual one-down position.

7. You, too, will have to get used to an unpredicta-

ble life in which you and your husband work out your tasks, your plans, your goals together instead of accepting them secondhand from television shows or your friends and family.

Of course, for women too these "losses" are just the reverse side of what you have to gain:

1. In sharing the breadwinning or being prepared to do so, you will also share the rewards and pleasures which can come from having a job: you can enjoy an increased income; and, even if you never work at an income-producing job but are always prepared, you will have the security of knowing that you will not starve if something happens to your husband.

2. In sharing household chores and child care with your husband, you will have more free time to spend with your husband or to use in other involvements. You will find that your children are more emotionally healthy for having two parents who are not overburdened with child care but who both are involved with the children.

3. By sharing decision-making, you will find that you have a sense of being in control of your life, that you will not build up resentment against your husband for decisions that do not go right, since you shared in making the decisions.

4. By asking for what you want in a straight way and by not getting your way or winning arguments with emotionalism, you will have greater respect for yourself.

5. In developing your strength and competence with mechanical things, you will feel more secure

when your husband is not available or if something should happen to him, and you will gain further self-respect the more you can do things for yourself.

6. If you leave the pedestal, you will know you are respected for yourself and not for your sex alone. You will no longer be patronized by being allowed on the pedestal in public and on Mother's Day while being kept in a one-down position most of the time.

7. You have the choice of whether to work so that if you choose to be a full-time homemaker and mother, you will not have been forced into the role but will have chosen it freely and so will not resent it.

8. You are more likely to enjoy your children as individuals if they are not your responsibility solely and if they are not the only source of your fulfillment.

9. If you work outside you will no longer have to feel responsible for doing a second full-time job as homemaker when you return from your paying job.

10. When you give up the security of a predictable life, you too will find that your marriage and your life are adventures, that both you and your husband will be more creative and will inspire each other to lead more creative lives.

By choosing to have an equal marriage, parents also gain an additional benefit for their children.

You'll have the satisfaction of knowing that you are giving your daughters and sons their full humanity, without limitations according to sex. Your daughters will know they are free to take up the profession they choose without being limited to a few "women's" careers. Your sons will accept household chores as a natural part of a man's life. Your children will be prepared not only for their own equal marriage and equal parenthood but for those periods of their lives when they are single and must take care of themselves completely.

There are also a few things many people fear they will lose in an equal marriage which they will not lose.

1. Their masculinity or femininity, though it will remain intact, will be redefined.

2. Their sexuality will not disappear. Although *Esquire* and other magazines have blamed an "epidemic" of impotence on liberated women, there has been no proof that impotence is becoming more common or that it is due to women's gaining equality. Impotence often may be a problem within a couple's relationship, but Masters and Johnson and others have found that it is most often caused by the man's having too high an expectation of himself. Some unliberated men may be threatened by liberated women and thus doubt their own potency, but men who are liberated from the straight jacket of prescribed masculine behavior will be complimented rather than threatened if a woman initiates sex or if she enjoys it, and they will not feel pressured to a superhuman performance, as demanded by the masculine mystique.

It's a toss-up what is supposed to happen to women's sexuality when marriage becomes equal and they have a choice in the matter. At a press conference on women's rights, two male reporters stopped a female reporter and asked if she believed in equality for women. When she said yes, one of them said if women got equality men would never get their wives to have sex with them again. The other man asked the woman, who was married, if she would go to bed with him. Some people seem to think women hate sex and are being forced into it by their subservient relationship, while others seem to think women are sex fiends who must be dominated to be kept sexually faithful.

The reality is that some women might choose to have more and some women less sex if given an opportunity to tell their husbands what they want. Either way, it would be better sex, being voluntary, with women being free to express themselves and to take some of the initiative.

3. Men's status will not be lowered by having a wife who is an equal. Most people are impressed with a two-profession family. If not, then they will probably be impressed with the material goods two incomes can provide. If a wife is not working but the husband shares the evening and weekend household duties, most people will think highly of him for being a considerate husband, even if they do not understand that the work is equally his.

Even if you are one of those people who deliberately chose a spouse you believed to be inferior to you, there are reasons why you should still make your marriage an equal relationship:

1. Most people have some areas in which they excel. Even if you have many areas in which you have more knowledge and ability, it will benefit the whole family if your spouse brings different skills and knowledge to those areas in which she or he has more experience. Having responsibility in some areas will

allow your spouse to grow in self-confidence and ability in other areas as well.

2. Considering your spouse as an equal does not say that every idea she or he has and suggestion he or she makes is just as good as every idea and suggestion of yours, but the consideration does allow each idea to be judged on its own merit.

3. If you accept your spouse as an equal, you will both be free to discuss your feelings as unequals never are. Even if you aren't intellectual or social equals, you can be emotional equals.

4. Your children have much to gain by seeing both parents function as real parents, after whom they can model themselves, and from having a real relationship with their father as well as their mother on a day-to-day basis.

5. You must have had some interest in your spouse or you wouldn't have married. Sharing the responsibilities of marriage will give you more in common and will free your spouse to spend a little time at the activities—be they reading, a hobby, or applying makeup—which used to make your spouse interesting to you.

6. If you don't treat your spouse as another child but allow your spouse to be responsible for herself or himself, your spouse will not become a burden to you, and you will not have to worry about what would happen to your family if you were incapacitated or dead.

What if a man is working full time and the wife is a full-time housewife? Can't he then feel justified in letting her do all the household chores and child care as part of her job since he does his job of bringing home the money?

According to the U. S. government, a housewife works ninety hours a week. Sometimes it is hard to see that she has been working all day, since much of her work is undone by the cooking of the next meal or by messy children. Some of her tasks don't show, like chauffeuring children, answering the telephone, and listening to the children's problems. Others are taken for granted, like shopping for groceries. But it all adds up to a workweek that is more than twice as long as the average paid worker's.

You really have a choice of either watching your wife put in the equivalent of another workweek while you are at home or sharing the load to get it done in half the time and being able to do things together.

It all boils down to rethinking the purpose of marriage. If your reason for getting married is to have your clothes washed, as well as having someone to wait on you and provide sex when you want it, then you are hiring a servant. Most of those services can be contracted for outside of marriage at a higher cost ($790 a month, the government estimates), but it is more honest than marrying a woman to make her a servant.

Few women these days will agree to such a utilitarian marriage—few have to sell themselves into bondage just to survive. Most people now marry because they enjoy each other's company and want to be together and to raise a family together. Such a marriage of friends becomes a utilitarian exchange of services for financial support only gradually, after the first child is born and/or the couple's interests grow in different directions. When people decide for equality in marriage, they are asking to reverse that process or to prevent it from ever happening. Marriage is humanity's best refuge from loneliness, but only if it is a true partnership.

CHAPTER 3
COMMITMENT AND EQUALITY

How will equality in marriage change your life? Will it mean going in separate ways? An end to fidelity? Could it even come to the wife's abandoning her husband and children, as we see played up on television and in newspapers and magazines these days?

Equality means equal rights to develop as persons and equal responsibilities for taking care of ourselves, each other, and our children. It doesn't mean an absolute 50-50 split of the work. That is impossible and treats only the symptoms, not the attitude on which equality depends.

In an equal marriage, each partner is responsible for the health of the marriage. If the husband does something the wife considers detrimental to the marriage—stays away from home too much, flirts with a woman at a party, doesn't do the chores he has agreed to do, or spends too much money—that doesn't mean the wife has an equal right to stay out, flirt, slack off, and overspend. She has the responsibility of talking straight to her husband, telling him what effects his actions are having and asking him to change (and getting help from a marriage counselor if things are not resolved).

Equality means the end of defining each other by sex roles; neither husband nor wife can be predicted or assigned certain jobs because "he is the man" or "she is the woman."

Equal marriage means taking the wants, needs, talents, skills, likes, and dislikes of the husband and wife into consideration when deciding who will do which job. The best cook will do most of the cooking, but not all. And neither will want to do some jobs. They may want to trade jobs they like for those they don't—the wife may trade cooking, which she likes and the husband doesn't, for vacuuming, which she hates and he can tolerate. If both like to garden, they may decide to do it together as a kind of hobby.

Problems most likely arise with those jobs both detest. Traditional couples try to claim those jobs "belong" to the other sex, as did the couple who wrote the advice columnist to ask, "Is it the man's job or the woman's job to take out the garbage?" Equal partners realize that it is the couple's job, and they must decide on a fair way to get the garbage taken out, or if they can afford it, hire someone to do it.

June, a widow of a traditional marriage, talks constantly about how much she misses David, but the things she misses are his gardening and doing household repairs which she now has to pay to get done. She never mentions personal characteristics of his or their companionship as what she misses, just his function as "the man of the house."

In such traditional marriages, the husband is a representative of the male sex and the wife is the representative of the female sex. They ignore their own personalities and strive to fit the pattern of how a husband and wife are supposed to behave. They may not start out as a typical man and a typical woman, but they mold each other to fit the stereotypes.

Back when David and June were young, she didn't fit the wifely mold to his satisfaction. She wasn't a neat housekeeper. So one Sunday morning when David's buddies came to get him to play golf, he told them he couldn't go because he had to clean up the bedroom where his bride had been piling clothes for a month. The buddies laughed at the thought of David's doing "women's work" and at June's being incompetent at it. Word spread to all their friends, and June was humiliated, ready to leave him. But she had no money except what David provided, and when she called her father, he agreed with David that June had to learn her place, so he refused to send her money.

In an equal marriage, such humiliation would never take place, and couldn't, since there is no such thing as "women's work." Husband and wife work as a team. The important thing is that the team gets ahead, no matter what the game. Every player does as much as possible to see to it that the team wins, contributing whatever he or she can. A family must have enough money, a reasonably clean house, cooked meals, and cared-for children. It doesn't matter who does these things but that they get done so that each partner will have time to spend with the other and with their children, for reading and studying, for community work, for hobbies, or for whatever they want to do.

Equal marriage partners would never have to resort to humiliating each other to get their way either. Embarrassing or criticizing a spouse lowers both of you in other people's opinion—Why did she marry him if he's such a slob?—and tends to reinforce the spouse's bad habits—the guy who occasionally drops his socks on the floor hears his wife telling him he "always" does it and starts to think of himself as a person who always drops socks. Equal partners work on problems with each other instead of complaining to friends.

Equality in marriage does not mean lack of commitment, although many people believe it does, ever since the publication of Nena and George O'Neill's book *Open Marriage.* Their belief that in an open marriage "new possibilities for additional relationships exist . . . [and that] these outside relationships may, of course, include sex" seems to allow affairs, as both partners are free to have them. They do not recommend outside sex, but they "are not saying that it should be avoided, either" (pp. 253-54).

Because of that statement, open marriage has come to be synonymous with adulterous marriage, to the point that an ad for a recent movie, *I Could Never Have Sex with Any Man Who Has So Little Regard for My Husband,* stated that it was a film about "that growing group of married couples who still resist the idea of an open marriage, but who like to try leaving it ajar."

We don't believe there is any room for sexual experiments with other partners in a good marriage. When a person marries, he or she is choosing a deep sexual relationship and renouncing the variety of more superficial relationships available to single people. The partners promise to concentrate their efforts on that one relationship. People with full lives do not have unlimited sexual energy, and they are deceiving themselves if they think they can satisfy a spouse and someone else, too. Usually, "cheating" in marriage means the partner is cheated out of a satisfying sexual relationship.

The most dangerous aspect of adultery is that it involves being dishonest, when a good marriage requires honesty. It generally requires lying about where you have been and whom you have been with, and it means blocking off a whole set of experiences from sharing with your spouse. Since the whole point of marriage is breaking down the barriers between two persons so that they can be open and intimate with each other, extramarital sex and the barriers it creates are a blow to the heart of a marriage.

Of course some couples claim to have an "understanding," often including an agreement not to talk about what they have done, which really means they have gone into the relationship planning to hold back on complete commitment to the spouse.

Sex has been blown out of proportion in our society, with every ad using it to sell and every movie plot turning on it and pseudo discussion of it over most coffee cups. At the same time that it has been considered so important that no one should have to go without it, sex has been trivialized to the level of food and going to the bathroom. But it isn't like that at all. Sex does bind people together. Sex isn't everything in marriage or even a large share of it, but a marriage without adequate sex begins to unravel. Further, a couple with only a sexual relationship and nothing else in common may find that there is soon more to the relationship than they originally intended—that with this bond they are becoming "involved."

An acquaintance of ours once chose a man quite different from her in social status, financial level, attractiveness, and social graces with whom she believed she could have a purely sexual relationship. Although they had little in common except sex and knew they were using each other, both of them developed longings for a relationship that was more than one-dimensional. They began arguing bitterly over which way they wanted the relationship to grow. Despite many attempts, they found it difficult to end the relationship until finally the woman became sexually involved with another man and was able to break off the first relationship. Sex is hard to isolate from the rest of your life.

Sex also takes time. Finding and courting and having intercourse with a person outside the marriage takes a good deal of time, more than it would inside the marriage. That time is being taken away from spouse, children, or job. Everyone alive has only 168 hours a week. He or she may choose the way these hours will be spent, but a job takes 40 plus commuting time; sleep takes about 56; eating, dressing, and household chores take a good many; and each person, especially in a partnership, has only a few discretionary hours to use in activities with the spouse and children, community activities, hobbies, and recreation. Something has to give. Time spent relating to an outside romantic interest has to come from somewhere.

The O'Neills (*Open Marriage*) were wrong about time, not only time for outside sex but also leisure time. Although they are correct that married couples can't be all things to each other all the time, they do need a great deal of time together in order to be as many things to each other as they can. The O'Neills were undoubtedly trying to break the notion of "togetherness" so popular in the fifties, the idea that a couple and later their children had to do everything together. Still, having dinner, going to concerts, and playing chess with friends instead of the spouse, or going to parties and art exhibits alone and meeting each other at the end of the day to talk about what you have done separately goes against the grain of marriage. People marry each other because they want to spend more time together than they can just dating; following the open-marriage formula, they may well spend less time together. Two persons who have enough in common to get married will be able to spend most of their time in mutually enjoyable activities.

Everyone will have some interests that are not shared, but they still need not always keep the couple apart. One couple we know shares a den with his model airplane tools and her sewing table side by side so they can talk and share their accomplishments while pursuing different hobbies. Another husband likes Sunday afternoon football, while his wife likes to read the paper. They do both because he wears headphones to watch the game while she sits next to him reading the paper. Then they can share interesting bits of articles and exciting instant replays without imposing on each other. Earplugs are another good device for putting noncompatible activities together.

Sometimes it is inevitable that a couple must either do things separately or not at all. One physical fitness fiend is married to a woman who is a bit overweight and not keen on exercise. She goes with him on easy hikes, but in order for him to take a challenging hike occasionally, they plan several weekends a year that he will go on Sierra Club outings while she stays home and does some of the things she likes but he doesn't. She also sleeps late on Sundays while he takes twenty-mile bicycle rides and comes home to wake her up. Then they spend the rest of the day together.

These solutions are in the tradition of open marriage, but the difference is that they are considered second-best solutions by the participants, who would prefer to be together, rather than considered an ideal way to run a marriage. Marriage is not just different-sex roommates sharing the same bedroom and little else. It is sharing a life; time and how it is used are what make up a marriage.

Many people believe commitment means loss of freedom when it means the opposite. Once a person chooses a partner for life, she or he becomes free to be friends with the other sex just as naturally as with the same sex. The flirtations and signals and games that single people use to encourage or discourage each other are gone when there is no possibility of seduction. Only friendship remains. New possibilities for nonsexual friendships with the other half of humanity open up.

CHAPTER 4
WHO'S THE BOSS?

Traditional wisdom says that the man must be the boss in a happy household. Obviously that is not compatible with equal marriage. Decisions must be made in any family, so how *do* they get made when the spouses are equal?

In any marriage, decisions are made either by the husband or by the wife or they are made jointly. In a patriarchal or matriarchal marriage, one partner makes all major decisions and leaves only trivial decisions to the mate. Two solutions remain to those who want equality. They may either make all important decisions jointly, or they may designate some decisions as those to be made by the husband and an equal group of decisions as those to be made by the wife.

Parceling out an equal number of decisions to each spouse ensures equality, but not intimacy, and it does not guarantee that both spouses will be happy with all decisions. Joint decisions require more time and thought, but they build intimacy in the marriage, and both spouses will be more content with the decisions made.

Whichever way the couple chooses to make its decisions, it is important that both spouses know where they stand. Many arguments and much undermining of marriages is caused by spouses' usurping the making of those decisions that were not clearly designated as joint or as belonging to the other spouse.

Clearly we favor joint decision-making, but how do decisions get made when neither spouse has the ultimate authority? Much of the time it is quite easy. Having similar backgrounds and values as a basis for their marriage to begin with, the spouses will arrive at a similar conclusion independently, and there will be no disagreement.

If they do not agree they will try persuasion, each stating all the reasons her or his suggestion should be accepted. If either is persuaded, the problem is solved. If not, they must compromise.

Compromise, rather than being a restriction, can be one of the most creative aspects of marriage. Instead of acting on the first solution offered, the couple must think of all solutions each offers and decide which one both can live with.

A couple choosing tile for the kitchen floor may both choose the same pattern instantly, or one can persuade the other that his or her choice is best. If not, they may either continue shopping until they find a third pattern both consider acceptable, or they may each give a little—she may agree to the design he prefers if they order it in the color she prefers.

The more the couple cares about a decision and the greater their expertise, the more difficulty they may have in making the decision. An architect and a design artist had a fairly easy time designing and building their new house: she made suggestions according to her concept of design, but he, the architect, clearly had more expertise in the execution. But when it came to furnishing the new house, they deadlocked. Both knew a great deal about decorating and furnishing and both cared intensely that their home should be impeccable and a true reflection of their taste and professional ability. It took them a year and a half of shopping and discussion to choose a couch for the living room. After that, decorating was easier because they used the couch as the focus for the room and because they had worked out a process for compromise which carried over to other decisions.

It may seem that this is a complex way to decide, but it is really less disruptive than one person's having his or her own way. If one person decides, the other will resent it, may even sabotage the decision so she or he can say "I told you it wouldn't work," and may become involved in devious schemes to change the decision. The old television comedy "I Love Lucy" was typical of this. The plot usually called for Ricky to make a decision—not to buy a house, not to take Lucy to Europe with him—and called for Lucy to spend the rest of the show scheming to reverse the decision. Instead of lovers, they became adversaries. It finally becomes difficult to love the person who is constantly thwarting or opposing you, and such a marriage decays. Unfortunately, old television shows don't decay but are rerun over and over to give new generations of children horrifying concepts of how marriage "works."

Being the one to make a decision isn't always a pleasure or privilege to be coveted. Making a decision means taking the risk of being wrong or of having the rest of the family upset with the result. It also means having to find out enough information to make an intelligent decision, which takes time and energy.

Bob and Susan were able to decide that they wanted to take their two children and go out to dinner on Friday nights after they had both finished their workweek, but their problem was in deciding on a restaurant. Both were tired and wanted to be relieved of the responsibility. Each week they would climb in the car and Bob would ask, "Where will it be?"

And each week Susan would respond, "I don't care, wherever you want. You're driving." They wound up spoiling the evening they had meant to enjoy by arguing over who would decide.

They finally reached a compromise that allowed them each to enjoy three weeks of not deciding and made their week of deciding something to look forward to. Bob, Susan, and both children each had a week in turn in which they would choose a restaurant. Everyone in the family clearly knew who was to decide, and each looked forward to the one Friday when she or he got the choice of a favorite place or a favorite type of food. By rotating, they assured themselves that no one could take the passive-aggressive–one-down position, letting the spouse decide so the other person could criticize and blame the spouse for anything wrong with the restaurant's food or service.

Money is one of the major areas of decision-making for any couple. Beyond bare subsistence, how money is spent is determined by the values of the spouses and by who is deciding. Whether to buy better cuts of meat and less expensive shoes or vice versa depends on what the marriage partners consider more important. In an equal partnership, they will have to come to a conclusion which both consider reasonable, or they will trade—meat one month, shoes the next.

However they do it, spending is *not* decided by who is earning the money. In an equal partnership the money belongs to the partnership, and both partners have an equal say in how it is spent. No special rewards are attached to being the "breadwinner," and a person who is not earning is never reduced to feeling like a charity case when he or she needs money for clothes or tuition or a roll of film. When times are hard, the whole family realizes that it must live austerely, and when times are good, everyone gets a little extra.

Traditionally, the husband's job has been the deciding factor in where the couple lives. Many people find it shocking to imagine that a wife would refuse to go with her husband when he is transferred or that a couple should decide to move to a town where the wife could get a better job; yet this is becoming more common in equal marriages. Pam, an organic chemist, wants a job teaching and doing research in a university, which is harder to find than the job her husband wants—anything connected with physics. So Pam sends her resumés all over the country and makes the trips for interviews while her husband stays home. When Pam finds the job she wants, her husband will begin his job hunt within commuting distance of her job.

Jack was disgusted with his job as a newspaper editor and decided to quit, expecting Mary, who worked at the same paper, to quit with him and move to a new city. He was surprised to learn that Mary did not want to quit and, in fact, wanted him to quit without angry words which might affect her relationships on the job. Mary told Jack she would be happy to support the family financially until he could find a new job in the same city but that she enjoyed her job and valued her friends in that city and would not consider moving. Jack thought over his long-range plans and realized he had always wanted to become a columnist. While Mary continued in her job, they cut their spending drastically and he began a column. Three years later, Jack is earning as much with his column as he had as an editor, and Mary has found another job in the same city, a job she likes even better.

More and more companies are finding that couples are not at their mercy any longer, according to a number of *Wall Street Journal* articles. Couples decide what they value most in life and make their decisions according to those priorities. If they value money, they move whenever the husband or wife gets a promotion tied in with a transfer. But if they prefer a certain part of the country or want to live near a beach or want to remain near their friends, they decide to limit themselves to jobs to be found in the area.

How to spend your money, where to live, how to raise your children, how to decorate your living room are decisions both spouses must be happy with because both will have to live with the results, so both will need to participate in deciding. Some other decisions allow more leeway because the spouse is not necessarily affected by the decision made. Who to choose as friends and what to do with your leisure time are decisions that may be made separately sometimes without affecting the spouse. It is nice to have friends you both like and enjoy doing things with, but it isn't necessary for both spouses to like all of each other's friends. If a husband can't stand his wife's best friend, the wife can arrange to have lunch with her friend, call her during the day, and not plan to see her when the husband will be involved and vice versa. Both spouses should feel free to plan occasional evenings at meetings or activities which do not interest the spouse. If the uninvolved spouse is given ample notice of the evening out, he or she will be able to plan to do some things the involved spouse would not enjoy—watch a television show the spouse dislikes, eat a dinner the spouse finds distasteful, or whatever she or he would enjoy. Spouses also need to leave time for each other to be alone for thinking, reading, writing, and any other activity that requires solitude.

Partners have no business telling their mates how to decorate their offices or other rooms which belong to the mate, how to spend small amounts of pocket money, how to dress, and how to think. Spouses certainly can influence each other in these areas with compliments, critiques, gifts, and suggestions, but the final decision in these more private matters is up to the one who is most affected.

Sometimes differences of opinion are due to temperament. Warm-blooded and cold-blooded people are never going to agree on a comfortable temperature for their homes, but they can compromise. Morning and night people will find they are at odds on bedtime and rising time as well as appropriate late-night and early-morning activities. Morning people hate parties and long movies at night and find it easy to argue with a spouse at night over something that wouldn't have bothered them in the morning. Night people hate breakfast and early work hours and are grouchy when they first get up. It can be quite advantageous having one of each in a marriage, however. The morning person can see the kids off to school and help the spouse get up, while the night person can wait up for any late teen-agers and turn off the television set the early riser will undoubtedly go to sleep in front of. While one person is crabby, the other should be enough in control to calm things down. One night person who had been married to another night person claimed, "We would never have gotten a divorce if we had just had the sense not to talk to each other at the breakfast table."

Many things newly married couples fight about they later find are just not worth fighting over. One young couple returned from a trip to Mexico with an armload of brightly colored paper flowers to liven up their cheap apartment but spent an hour arguing over how the flowers should be arranged. Finally one of them stuffed the flowers in a vase in disgust, and they agreed to do the arranging another day, after they cooled off. When they moved from the apartment two years later, the flowers had still not been arranged, but they had brightened the room anyway.

When compromise is necessary, spouses certainly can do it on an equal basis, just as they would if making a decision with a same-sex friend. The basis for making such compromises is having respect for each other and not questioning each other's basic integrity. Unfortunately, marriage has so grown over with myths and stereotypes that it is sometimes difficult for partners to see each other as real human beings. Equal partners must see past the labels "husband" and "wife" and interact with the unique personality they have married.

CHAPTER 5
HOUSEHOLD CHORES ARE THE ESSENCE OF EQUALITY

Hardly anybody likes cleaning house or washing clothes or grocery shopping or taking out the garbage or mowing the lawn.

You may have some things on that list that you hate more than others or some you would prefer to take on as your permanent responsibility so you could get out of others. But, on the whole, few people would prefer to do any of those chores over going to a movie, playing tennis, sailing, reading a good book, or listening to music. We would automatically question the sanity of anyone who claimed to wash clothes for a hobby, to spend free time shopping for groceries, or to "just love" taking out the garbage.

Yet household chores are basic to life and health, and we can't avoid them. We either do them ourselves or we con or pay someone else to do them for us.

Household chores—the things nobody really wants to do—often break an otherwise equal relationship.

No one who is trying to be equal would say, like a tradition-bound man, "Cleaning and shopping are women's work and they're beneath my dignity." No one who is trying to be equal would agree with the woman who let the yard go for three weeks while her husband was out of town because "I take care of the inside of the house, and he takes care of the outside."

Still, many people who are interested in equality find it hard to start participating in chores that once "belonged" to the other sex.

At UCLA's first women's rights day several years ago, a noon seminar on the changing role of women was held for men only. The men included a number of erudite professors and graduate students, men who should have been able to comprehend the subject, but the discussion died. Every time the group leader began discussing what he considered the agenda—how women's equality will change men's lives—the group changed the subject. When he asked such questions as "Who does the dishes at your house?" the scholars found that too mundane and changed to a discussion of more comfortable questions, such as "Can women be equal in a capitalistic society?" or "What will equal pay for women do to the American economy?" For them, as for many men and women, equality is something you talk about or even encourage at work, but living it every day in your home is too uncomfortable.

There is an easy out of sharing household chores, even if you do pay lip service to the idea of equality. Both sexes use the same escape route, but women have more to lose since there is much more housework that needs doing than yard and automobile work. But the favored escape is planned incompetence.

In the area of housework and shopping, men often point out that they took shop in school instead of home ec. They're really sorry, but the wife is so much better at household chores that she does them in much less time and with much greater skill.

On the other hand, a husband may actually try cleaning house or cooking a meal. But, since he has no background in the area, he fails so miserably that the wife declares his work hopeless and wades in to try to rescue the project, at which time he backs out.

Planned incompetence is a cop-out. We are all born totally incompetent at life, but we begin learning and we keep on learning new skills all our lives. Housework, yard work, mechanics, and even a new profession all involve teachable skills.

And men *must* learn homemaking skills for a relationship to be equal. A wife who has to do all the housework and child-care chores can't possibly be equal. She has no time for leisure activities which would make her a more interesting partner. If she works away from home at a paying job, she returns from it to another full-time job at home. She can't have time for the thinking, reading, planning, and extra projects that would lead to her getting promotions at work or to her getting what she really wants out of life. Not only will she have little to say to her husband, but she will have very little time to spend with him.

To ensure equality, both the husband and the wife must learn to do the jobs that were once assigned to the other sex. This was once billed as the "age of the specialist," but many people are coming to see that specializing is dehumanizing, whether it is in medicine or factory work, and many are going back to being generalists. Splitting your life into his and hers is dehumanizing because it alienates you from each other and makes you less capable of functioning as whole persons.

So, if you are like most people, you have a lot of skills to learn in order to end the artificial sex-role barriers between you and to make you fully capable of functioning in the world.

Actually, many of the skills you already have will help you with the new skills you are about to learn. Anyone who can run a vacuum cleaner can learn to use a lawn mower and vice versa. The person who can read and follow instructions for mixing a weed killer can learn to follow a recipe for a main dish. A person who knows how to change a baby can learn to change a tire. The woman who thinks she is totally unmechanical will find she knows a good deal about the way things work inside the house, and these apply outside. A man who does yard work and garage work will find he knows quite a bit about cleaning and straightening.

The important thing to remember is that no one does things perfectly the first time. Each of you will have to act as teacher for the other. Have patience and teach with love. If this were a casual date you were teaching to trim rosebushes, would you yell at her and take the pruning shears away? No, because she wouldn't have to take it. Point out how she could have done it better, praise the places where she did it right, and give her another chance—after all, the roses will grow back.

If this were your boyfriend cooking his first meal, would you be furious if he burned it? No, you'd praise the fact that he tried, eat whatever was edible, and sneak a peanut butter sandwich in the kitchen while no one was around. Spouses have as much need to be taught patiently and with love and encouragement as does any friend. Remember the first meal you cooked? Brides are notorious for their terrible cooking precisely because cooking is *not* a secondary female characteristic. Why should your husband's first efforts be any better?

And gardening and mechanics are not secondary male characteristics either.

Don't expect more the first time than you would from an intelligent child—after all, it was in childhood that each sex was cut off from the skills the other was taught.

Both partners may find they have trouble with the idea of the spouse's learning to do their job. People have a tendency to like to be thought of as indispensable, and if their partner could do their job the partner might be able to live without them.

No one is indispensable. Everyone is unique, and the job will be done in a different way. But the fact that your spouse is ignorant of certain skills only means she or he would have to depend on another person to do them, not that the tasks wouldn't be done at all. Far better to have the pleasure of doing things together, of not having either partner feel overworked, and of knowing that you each are there because you want to be, not because you couldn't survive without the other.

One way of sharing family responsibilities which has become popular in recent years is the marriage contract. All marriages are based on a contract written by the state and generally based on traditional concepts of the roles of men and women in marriage. It is a good idea to write down the basic principles that will govern your life together, as opposed to the principles the state tries to give you. If you aren't married yet, you may want to make these principles a part of your marriage vows. If you are already married, working them out together might help you see where you agree and disagree, where you need to do some negotiating.

Going into great detail is not a good idea, however. Some highly publicized marriage contracts spelled out how every aspect of the marriage will be run and have listed all jobs which must be done, with a schedule of who will do them and when. Such a contract ensures sharing, all right, but it can be so rigid that it takes all the spontaneity and fun out of the marriage.

If you agree in principle that you will share the household and child-care chores, that is part of your contract, and you should be able to trust each other to work out the details informally. You do need to agree on who will do what in general, but you need to be flexible so that if one person is swamped that person can ask for help.

For guidelines on negotiating changes in who does what in household chores, see chapter 9.

Just as the husband can learn to do the household chores, so can the wife learn to be an able breadwinner. Even if you have young children at home and both of you agree that the wife needs to stay home with them, she owes it to herself and to the family to take whatever training is necessary to develop her skills or keep them up so she will be ready to be the sole or co-breadwinner if she is needed.

The fact that every couple must face is that no matter how good your marriage is, no matter how much you want it to last, marriage is not forever. All marriages must end, whether in the death of one spouse or in divorce. Both spouses must be prepared for that time when they must live alone and perhaps support children. Social Security survivor's benefits or child support will keep you from starving, but they will not provide a comfortable living. Many men have thought they were leaving their families comfortable through their insurance and bank savings, but in a few years inflation has reduced their widows and children to near poverty. In cases of divorce, it is rare that a man can support two households comfortably, and, whether he marries again or not, he will have to provide two residences, at least two cars and food for two tables—a heavy burden.

In three cases out of four the woman outlives her husband. She and the children will have enough to adjust to without having to adjust to poverty as well. In divorce, the situation will be better for everyone if the adults can support themselves and share the support of any children.

Being prepared to share or take over the breadwinning is not just preparation for the end of the marriage, however. It will make life more secure and perhaps more fun during the marriage.

In times of economic crisis, different occupations are hit at different times. An aerospace worker who lost his job during the cutback in the space program was very glad that his wife, a newspaper reporter, could support the family during the two years it took him to find another job.

Having two job potentials makes it easier for either the husband or the wife to change jobs or to retrain for a different field. Tim, a scientist, was able to leave his job when he was given an assignment developing nuclear weapons, which he found objectionable, because he knew his wife, Susan, could support them with her job in chemistry until he could find a more acceptable position.

And, for that matter, Richard was able to leave a minister's position and train to be a marriage, family, and child counselor because Jean could support the family by teaching journalism.

Another good reason for both being prepared to work is that being a mother full time is not a permanent job. As much as you may wish that children would stay little and cuddly forever, they inevitably grow up. Many women find caring for an "empty nest" to be depressing, leading to a feeling that "nobody needs me." Often such women find that a career they can enter or return to will give them the sense of purpose in life that they would otherwise lack.

Money is another good reason for both working. If one can make a subsistence wage, two can make a comfortable income. If one can make a comfortable living, two can make possible some otherwise impossible luxuries.

Of course, many women work throughout their marriages, even with small children, because they like their work, find it fulfilling, and need or want the income.

What if the wife has a job that pays more money than the husband's job? In an equal partnership that is no problem. It simply means more income for the team. No special privilege is attached to earning money, so the husband will not lose status. A job seldom pays according to its value to society, so, whether the man or the woman earns more, the top earner can hardly conclude she or he is worth more. And even if one of the partners were valued more highly by society, that person gets no special treatment in the relationship. By choosing to be equals, they have chosen to obliterate any hierarchy dictated by society.

Don't confuse the word *share* with the word *help*. You are not being expected to help your wife with the housework, to help your husband by taking a full-time or part-time job.

The word *help* implies that it is still your wife's responsibility to keep house, your husband's responsibility to earn the living. And that is not equal.

The house must be kept clean and running. The living must be earned. These are duties of the *couple* in an equal marriage. You both track in dirt, wear clothes, and eat off the dishes, and you are both responsible for the cleaning up. You both live off the money that is brought in, and neither of you needs to feel more obligation because of sex to bring it in. You will decide as a couple how these responsibilities will be carried out.

CHAPTER 6
SEXUAL EQUALITY MEANS SEXUAL SATISFACTION

People aren't born knowing how to achieve a satisfying sexual relationship, just as they are not born knowing how to run a marriage. People look to traditions, myths, stereotypes, relatives, and peers to discover how marriage works. In the same way, they are guided in their sex lives by traditions, myths, stereotypes, and what their relatives and peers do and say. Each person uses all such information to form expectations of what marriage will be like long before ever meeting the partner. Each also forms expectations—well in advance—of what sex will be like, what role each will take, how often it will occur.

It is natural for people to try to anticipate what such an important step in their lives as marriage or such an important part of their lives as sex will be like, but by trying to live their expectations, to force each other into a preconceived mold, they rob their marriages of companionship and their sex lives of the pleasure they could have as equals.

Masters and Johnson point out that where once sex was something "done to" the woman and something which she did not enjoy, for many couples sex is now something "done for" the woman by her husband.

While the former was unfair to women the latter puts an unequal responsibility on the husband. Not only is he responsible for initiating sex, deciding what sex play the couple will engage in, and what position they will assume, but he is also the one who must take the blame if his wife does not have an orgasm or if he himself has problems with potency or can't reach a climax.

In an equal-partnership marriage, each spouse is responsible for his or her own satisfaction, with the cooperation of the partner, of course.

Either partner is free to initiate sex, and the spouse can feel free to say yes or (kindly) no. Seldom will two partners have the same need for sex. That drive is quite variable with health, fatigue, distraction, and whether a person has other ways of channeling creative energy. In an equal partnership it is *not* important that the couple have equal sex drives. Whoever wants more sex should ask for it more, and nobody should keep score. If you make it a rule that each of you will ask for sex if you want it, you will be able to prevent the guilt that many marriage partners, especially men, have developed from trying to second-guess their partner's needs: "I've been so tired this week that I haven't asked for sex. Is she (he) feeling frustrated? Does she (he) think I don't find her (him) attractive anymore? Does she (he) think I'm not much of a man (woman) if I don't want sex constantly?"

If you make it a rule that the person being asked for sex has the right to say no, you will avoid the "Am I asking too often?" second-guessing.

If you don't keep score, you can avoid the problem of taking turns which may lead to the feeling "I asked last time. I can't ask again this soon."

Of course the person being asked owes it to the other person to say yes if at all possible, since loving partners will want to fulfill each other's needs if they can.

You do need to make sure that your partner knows that you are asking. It is not uncommon for one partner to be angry at the spouse for "turning me down" only to discover that the other partner didn't realize what the signals meant. You don't necessarily have to say "How about having sex this afternoon at 2?" Many people are uncomfortable being that blunt, but you do need to talk about it and make sure you are either using the same terminology or that you each know the other's nonverbal signals—whether it be wearing certain nightclothes, playing a certain piece of music, or ringing a little bell.

You've probably noticed that we aren't making the automatic assumption that the husband will be the one wanting sex and the wife will be the one saying no. Neither sex has been well-served by these myths. Many men feel inadequate when they compare themselves to the myth of male supersexuality. In jokes, in stories, in everyday conversation, in movies, and on TV, men are made to seem constant sexual beings, ready to have sex with any young woman (as long as she is not physically deformed) at any time. Men are made to seem concerned only with the physical side of sex with no regard for emotional content. They are portrayed as faithful to their wives only out of fear of their wives, not out of emotional commitment to the marriage. A normal man is supposed to be always on the verge of an erection so that he is always immediately ready to have sex.

Real men aren't like that at all. Most of them are selective about who they have sex with, and that selection is normally based on the emotional relationship they have with a particular woman. Men usually choose to be faithful to their wives not out of fear, but out of a conscious choice to put the marriage first and give up any actions which might weaken that relationship. And normal men have times when they aren't at all interested in sex—times when they are tired or have their minds on something else.

Instead of reassurance from other men that it is normal to have ups and downs in your sex drive, to prefer sex with a woman you care for, and to be loyal to your wife, many men in their developing years get into "bull sessions" in which men try to outdo one another in telling of their sexual exploits, even though they are often lying. Far from being reassuring, such sessions may make the young man who believes what he hears feel inferior and inexperienced at sex, maybe even to the point of making up a few lies of his own.

It isn't hard to masquerade as a sexual superman in an unequal marriage. You can keep up the lies to other men, tell dirty jokes, and make sexual comments to the guys about women who pass by. You don't have to *do* anything, just talk. As for your wife, if she doesn't have the right to initiate sex, you can ask for it only when you feel rested and well and are not distracted, and she may believe that you are always ready to go and never have the need to be aroused.

That shouldn't happen in an equal marriage. Though you could keep up the front for other men, you have to be honest with your wife. If she wants sex and asks for it, you may have to turn her down because you just aren't up to it. Or you may be willing but may need her to kiss and caress you and stimulate your erogenous areas before you will be ready.

In an equal marriage, you must be honest about what you need. You will both have to learn what turns the other on. Men are just as likely as women to find that certain kinds of sex play turn them off. All male bodies are not sensitive in the same areas, and all female bodies do not have the same sensitivities. You need to try out different types of sex play and find out where your partner's body is sensitive. Discover what gives each other pleasure.

When you find out what turns your partner on and your partner finds out what turns you on, don't decide that that is permanently the answer. Keep trying new things. People aren't machines—you can't just learn what buttons to push to turn them on. As people grow and mature they may change from liking one thing to liking something they previously avoided. And people even find that different actions give them pleasure each time they participate in sex. A set routine quickly becomes monotonous and is a turn-off in itself.

In an equal marriage, each partner has the right to ask the other partner to engage in the kind of sex play that arouses him or her. Each partner also has the right to draw the line, to say "That repulses me" or "frightens me" or "hurts me" or "turns me off." But the other partner should not assume the line is drawn forever. As the relationship matures, the partner may find the suggestion that was once repulsive has become an exciting new dimension to what was becoming a routine sex life.

Women have no more escaped feelings of inferiority from hearing jokes and conversations about sex and from movies and TV than have men. From the same sources, they gather that only women with large busts can be satisfying sex partners. They learn that women are supposed to be passive in sex, so they begin to think themselves abnormal not to be able to have orgasm while lying quietly pinned to the bed. They are told that women are supposed to be turned on by the emotional elements of sex, but not by the physical. They come to believe that sex is a contest in which man is the conqueror and woman is the conquered, and they feel that, instead of being a gift they give each other, sex is something the woman must withhold from the man until she is secure and/or getting her way in other areas of life so that, when she "submits" and becomes the vanquished, she will at least have triumphed in another area of the relationship to counterbalance her "defeat."

Of course, all kinds of non–Miss-America types of

women have satisfying sex lives, and plenty of large-busted women have miserable sex lives because it isn't what kind of body you have, it's what kind of relationship you have with your partner and how you use the body you have that makes sex satisfying. But nice women don't talk much about sex at all, so they don't find out who is and isn't satisfied.

A few entrepreneurs have discovered in recent years that it was just a myth that women aren't turned on by male bodies. The nude centerfold of Burt Reynolds in *Cosmopolitan* started as a turn-about-is-fair-play retaliation, but that issue was almost instantly sold out, and other magazines began to grow rich by displaying much bolder male nudes. In fact, recent studies have shown that women are just as easily aroused by pornography as are men. Women just aren't the other-worldly creatures they have been portrayed as being.

Women like sex and want it as much as men. Sex is something partners do for each other. It is hard for many women not to feel conquered, after an adolescence in which their parents constantly cautioned them against letting boys take advantage of them. Perhaps one thing we could do for the next generation would be to make sure we teach both boys and girls that sex belongs in the context of a committed relationship and that they will lose self-respect and the respect of others if they rush into sex outside of such a relationship. Unfortunately, we have tended to teach only our girls to be cautious, while encouraging the boys to get away with as much sexual activity as they can—thus actually teaching our boys to act as though they had no responsibility for the relationship. Giving girls only the power to say no and boys the OK to try anything they want is no foundation for a future equal marriage in which both have the right to initiate and both have the right to say no.

When women feel they are "submitting" in sex, they come to think of sex as a favor they do for the man. But both sexes can be guilty of thinking of sex as a reward they give the partner for good behavior or as something to withhold if they do not get their way in something they wanted in another area of the relationship. Using sex to manipulate the spouse is not the same thing as saying no because you don't feel like having sex. Manipulation is not honest or legitmate, and it has no place in an equal marriage. Honestly not wanting to have sex is either partner's right.

Because of the myth of women's passivity, as well as a confusion of sex with wrestling, the idea is still popular that the person on top during sex is the dominant one in the relationship. Those who believe this think that the man's masculinity is threatened if his wife is on top during sex. Nonsense! The person on top has the most freedom of movement and can most easily have an orgasm. In the old days, when women were believed to not like sex anyway, the man could get it over with faster if he were on top. Most people need to be free to move without the weight of another person on them in order to be satisfied. And, as for women's passivity, most women find that their own motions are as much a turn-on as what the partner does.

A myth that is an easy trap for both partners in an equal marriage is the myth of simultaneous orgasm. It sounds so egalitarian. D. H. Lawrence built the myth up to be so attractive in *Lady Chatterly's Lover* when he had both partners losing consciousness at the same moment and coming to an almost mystical union because they reached their orgasms together.

However, for most couples simultaneous orgasm doesn't work. What does work is for the woman to be satisfied first, if for no other reason than because women are capable of multiple orgasms and men are not. If you aim for simultaneous orgasm, the man will have his and the woman will have one, which may be only half or a fifth or a tenth of her potential, depending on the woman and how she feels.

Aiming for simultaneous orgasm also means that neither partner can really concentrate on giving the other pleasure because an orgasm is possible only when concentrating on one's own feelings. In taking turns, each partner gets a chance to feel pleasure without holding back or trying to rush to keep up with the other, and each also gets the chance to give the partner pleasure and to enjoy the partner's response.

Taking turns can also solve the problem of who should be on top. If you are taking turns, the person who needs the freedom of being on top can be on top. You can begin with the woman on top and, when she is satisfied, roll over and give the man his turn.

Equal partners share the responsibility for their sex life, and so they don't "blame" anyone if things go wrong. They simply talk things out and try doing things differently. If they can't solve the problem, they can go to a marriage counselor for help.

Sometimes the problem is one of a night person's being married to a day person. The night person may assume sex is something you do at bedtime, while the day person is too weary to function well then but wakes up in the mornings ready to go. No matter how extreme the problem is for you, there are bound to be some hours during which you both have an energy level that is sufficient. Whether you find the best time is early evening or high noon, do it then.

"But what about the children?" you may wonder. With tiny children, any hour of the day or night may be a problem. They may need immediate attention anytime, and one of you must find out what is wrong. So you might as well take your chances on earlier hours as later. Older children who are self-sufficient may be told that they are not to disturb their parents when a Do Not Disturb sign is on the bedroom door. Eventually they will figure out that it means their parents are having sex. In the long run it will be quite healthy for them to realize that sex is an important part of your relationship.

Another problem most married couples have to face at some time is the long absence, illness, or incapacitation of one of them. They may feel the lack of sex acutely. Literature, folklore, and common knowledge is full of wandering husbands and wives who were faithful until the spouse was absent or ill or giving birth, and the person needed sex and so turned to a third person.

That doesn't have to happen. If your spouse is present but ill or not capable of having sex, you can maintain your closeness with touching, with talking, and by assuring each other of your love. At a distance you can still keep the relationship going by telephone and letter. That, of course, will never take the place of sex, and, in fact, it is only when you are deprived of sex that you come to feel the greatest need for it. You don't have to be unfaithful, though. Masturbation can give you the physical relief you need under such circumstances, and it won't harm your relationship or risk hurting a third person or bringing home V.D. It isn't a cure-all, however, for unsatisfactory sex lives. It should never be used instead of talking over your problems and working out a more satisfactory sexual relationship.

Sex is important to a marriage, but partners must never confuse sex with affection. Affection is the lifeblood of a committed relationship. It is the hugs and kisses and winks and pats that tell you that you are the most important person in your partner's life. Neither partner ever gets too much of that kind of assurance. When people confuse sex and affection, they mistake every affectionate gesture as a come-on for sex. Small wonder that they discourage their spouses from the constant giving of affection. They are not prepared for it to continue into intercourse that often. Use separate signals so you can give and receive lots of affection without worrying that it will always lead to sex. When sex is what you want or *becomes* a desire as a result of affection, send a different signal so your partner can freely move into sex or decline.

Our society has put such emphasis on sex that we sometimes substitute it for affection, success, or creativity. Sex wasn't meant to take the place of any other satisfactions in life; its function is to add to all the other satisfactions and to strengthen the bond of commitment.

CHAPTER 7
EQUALITY OF PARENTHOOD

Children are known to profit from having both parents involved with them, yet children in this century have been left for mother to raise while father went to work to support them.

The child whose father is too busy or too "masculine" to be involved in daily child care loses some things that are important. A boy neglected by his father doesn't get a chance to experience the fact that father feels good about being a man, and he may come to feel that it is better to be a woman. A girl who grows up neglected by her father does not get his affirmation that women are fine people and that he enjoys her company. She may always think of men as strange creatures foreign to her if she doesn't get the chance to learn with her father how to relate to men. This affirmation of sex is the only reason children need a parent of each sex, and it is the reason single parents need to provide other-sex adults for their children. Given such affirmation, there is no reason why a single-parent home cannot be as healthy as a two-parent home.

However, having a two-parent home with only one parent involved with the children can be devastating. Children need to have both parents involved in a two-parent home because they will take a parent's lack of involvement as a rejection of them, and they may live their whole lives trying to win the approval and acceptance of the "rejecting" parent.

Having two adults in the home also gives children other advantages. Two persons will automatically have more time than one, so the children will have more attention. Each adult will bring a unique set of skills and behaviors and ways of relating, and the children will have more possibilities to choose from in selecting behavior patterns. Every child will relate to each parent in a different way, finding one parent the person to talk to about one kind of problem and the other parent right in a different situation.

The real winners in equal parenting, however, are the parents, especially the father. Many fathers and their children have become strangers to each other. It is only through constant, deep involvement in a child's life that you become its true parent. That involvement consists mostly of doing little things for and with the child, not just in roughhousing or an occasional game.

Our society has managed to evolve a family structure that gave Mother no outlet for her talents and energies except raising children, while pushing Father out into the world and denying him his children. Father found he had to commute long distances to work, and it was the children's bedtime shortly after he got home. He may have found that society more highly rewarded him for being "married to his job," putting all his creativity, devotion, and time in the job instead of the family. He may also have found that Mother resented his "intruding" in her domain of home and children. If she had no other options open to her, what right did he have to get involved with the children who were *her* creation? Didn't he have his work? Social critics have said our children are being overmothered. They could just as easily have described it as being underfathered, but rigid sex roles which divide the parents' roles into two separate worlds are the cause of the problem.

Equal parenting means the relationship must be redefined. The children belong to both of you equally. They are equally your responsibility, obligation, burden, and joy.

In an equal marriage a father's right to parent his children is as inalienable as the mother's. In a patriarchal home, Father was a distant figure, but he had great authority. While he did not know his children well and did not have a warm relationship with them, he always got his way by demanding it. In a nonpatriarchal home, in which the parents have an equal marriage, Father loses his appeal to authority and must have a genuine, close relationship with the children in order to influence them.

Men are often told that little babies are women's province, but a baby whose father keeps hands off will learn that Mother is the reliable one, and Mother will be the major influence on the child.

In the past, fathers *were* involved in their children's lives. Farm families worked in the fields, ate three meals a day together, had both parents available to answer questions or solve a crisis. Shop owners lived behind the store and used their children as assistants, and craftspeople often taught their sons and daughters their trade. That doesn't necessarily mean the parents had equal partnership marriages, but at least both of them were deeply involved in parenting.

Today people who like children enough to have them will want to share with each other the satisfactions of watching a baby grow into a child, a child into an adult.

Except for breast-feeding, no child-care chores automatically belong to one sex or the other. Either parent can diaper, bottle feed, dress, or soothe an infant, and either can tie shoes for, transport, pack lunch for, discipline, or listen to an older child. If children are important enough to have and to support, they are important enough to spend time with.

Anyone who does not want to spend time with children or share in the child care should not become a parent. Parenthood, in these days of access to birth control and abortion, is not automatically a part of marriage. Children are a joint responsibility even before they are born.

Before deciding whether to have a child, couples need to consider realistically what is involved. Time for children must come from somewhere, so prospective parents must realize they will have to give up some of their present activities. Some may feel they have time by cutting out television and nights on the town, but others may fear that children will usurp their time together.

Parents do have much less time alone together than do childless couples. Much of the time when they are together the children will be in the same room, so they will lack privacy. If one spouse is used to being "babied" by the other, he or she may fear that parenthood will mean the baby gets all the babying and none will be left for the spouse.

Partners must decide that their marriage comes first, ahead of the children. This is important for the children as well as the parents because the home is built on the foundation of the parents' marriage, and if the marriage crumbles, the children will suffer.

That means that before you bring children into your home, you agree to guard your time together and make it meaningful, that if either partner feels the need to talk to the other privately the children who are old enough to understand are asked to leave you alone for a time, and that you make it clear that parents have the right to expect some babying from each other if they want it, but the one who wants it must take responsibility for making that wish clear to the spouse in some way.

If you feel you can't live with restrictions on your time, privacy, and attention given to each other, then parenthood is not for you. If you can, there are other factors to consider.

Can you afford a child? Delivery costs have soared along with hospital rates, and adoption costs along with attorney's fees. Once you have the child, it is one more mouth to feed, body to dress, mind to educate, and maybe additional housing costs. You will have a lower standard of living for yourself if you have children.

Are you prepared for the extra work required for a young child—washing, bathing, dressing, preparing food, changing diapers, teaching, and listening? The work is much less straining if shared between the parents, of course.

Are you prepared to have your freedom restricted? Parents can't just decide to go to a movie or out to dinner on the spur of the moment. They must see to it that a responsible person is in charge of their children at all times. Again, equal parents have the advantage because, even if they cannot go out together without arranging for a baby-sitter, at least they each have the right occasionally to go alone to a meeting or class or on an errand without feeling they are shirking their duty in leaving the other parent with the children. An equal mother does not have to become a prisoner of her baby, as sometimes happens in homes where the father feels he has no responsibility for child care.

Are you ready to be a parent instead of a child yourself? Many people find it more comfortable to be the one being controlled and taken care of rather than to control and take care of a child. People who have been out of childhood only a short time often find they feel resentful of their children. One woman who had her children when she was still a teen-ager found herself competing with her fifteen-year-old daughter because the mother was still young and attractive at thirty and had missed out on the dances and dates she saw her daughter starting to enjoy. The relationship was uncomfortable for both the mother and the daughter. Have you gotten to do all the things you hoped to do which will be difficult with children? If you haven't, you can do almost anything you want—foreign travel, backpacking, finding all the out-of-the-way good restaurants in town, changing careers—but it will be more difficult and will require more advance planning than if you were childless.

If you've considered all these factors and you want to have a child or another child and you want to be equal parents, you've still got some planning to do. Who is going to take care of the child? In an equal marriage, the answer isn't automatically Mother.

Later you can find good child-care centers for toilet-trained children, but infant care is hard to find, and you may want to be there yourselves in the baby's early months or years. You need to think about your jobs. Does one of you want to stay home, and could you afford the loss of income? Could you each take a cut in the number of hours you work and arrange your schedules so each stayed home with the baby part time? Do your jobs provide for maternity and paternity leave? Could one or both of you take the baby to work with you?

If you decide that one of you will stay home, you also need to provide social, professional, community, and/or recreational contacts for that person, whether the employed spouse stays home with the child or you hire a baby-sitter. An infant is not very stimulating company for months at a time. Both parents need to get out among adults frequently to keep their sanity and to keep growing themselves.

If you can juggle your hours so you each work at

least part time and take turns staying home, you'll both enjoy the benefits of a close relationship with your child and the stimulation of going out to work.

If you are entitled to maternity and paternity leaves, you may be able to take turns staying home full time and working full time.

If you decide to take the baby to work, you'll be a pioneer in returning to the way many of our ancestors raised their children. The world of work and the world of children have not always been so strictly separate, and many a child has had a first-hand knowledge of how its parents earned a living because the child was tied to the parent's back or played in a crib in the corner during working hours. Some jobs work better than others for taking baby along, and those where the baby could get hurt or where a high degree of concentration is required at all times would not be suitable. Even in those kinds of jobs, employers are increasingly coming to realize that employees will be happier and more dedicated to the job if they know their children are safe and well cared for and nearby, so they are beginning to provide child care at work. That way the parent can work undistracted but can visit the child during lunch hour, can be there in case of emergency, and can enjoy commuting regularly with the child.

What will you do if a child is sick? In an equal marriage, both parents' jobs are equally important. The wisest decision would be based on which of you could get away to be with the child. But, if you are both busy, who will give up the day of work? If it is automatically the mother, you aren't functioning as equal parents.

Parents also need to consider their other children, if any. What can you do to help them not feel threatened by the new baby or child? You may want to space the children farther apart to give each time to be "the baby" or have them close together to be companions. You may want to stop at one, and there is no reason why you shouldn't. Only children do not necessarily lead the lonely lives they have been portrayed to since they can have their parents' full attention and the neighbors' children to play with. You may want to investigate techniques for determining the sex of your next child or adopt a child so that you have one of each sex. Or you may choose to have your second child the same sex as the first if you have limited housing and want the children to share a room.

How many children to have will be a joint decision, one you will want to base on your income, energy level, population considerations, plans for your lives, and traditions families have followed.

What if one of you wants children and the other doesn't or one wants more children than the partner wants? Talk it over, trying to hear and understand the reluctant one's misgivings and to figure out how these misgivings can be cleared up. If, after you have thoroughly discussed the reluctant partner's misgivings, you can't come to an agreement that both spouses are enthusiastic about, then see a marriage counselor for help. If one of you just gets tired of the argument and gives in without feeling good about the decision, you may carry a resentment that will make the marriage unlivable in the future. If one of you does not want children but gives in to keep the other happy, the children lose by having a parent who resents their existence and will not be able to avoid communicating that fact to the chidren, often in subtle but powerful ways. If one gives in and agrees not to have children, that person may become bitter and regretful as the age for having children passes. Be honest with each other about your motivations for wanting or not wanting a child. Then get professional help if you are deadlocked.

If you decide to have children or you already have all you want, it is important for both parents to keep in mind that parenthood is a temporary job. The average family consists of two children, who rapidly grow past the total dependency of infancy. From toddlerhood on, children are capable of helping with their own care and starting to make independent decisions. By adolescence, they should be functioning as novice adults—be capable of caring for themselves and helping with family chores, making most of their own decisions with counsel of their parents, lacking only the ability to support themselves while they finish their education. Only a few years of an adult's seventy years of life will be spent taking care of dependent children. For that reason, neither parent should plan to make parenthood a life's career.

Parenthood is also a part-time job. True, an infant needs a great deal of care, but after that stage, children need space. They don't want a parent looking over their shoulders all the time. They need to know they can do some things all by themselves.

No parent should plan to get all his or her fulfillment in life from being a parent. That is too much of a burden for children to bear.

The primary goal of parenthood is to take a helpless infant and turn it into a fully functioning, independent human being.

Parents must always keep that goal in mind. A parent who forgets and begins to make parenting the thing that gives life meaning or one who thinks parenthood is permanent and full time and so neglects to find meaningful involvement in other things as the children grow in independence may be tempted to prolong the parenting phase by babying the child, by avoiding giving the child responsibilities suitable for her or his competence, or by keeping the child from going out in the world.

Parenting is at first largely physical—the feeding, diaper changing, bathing, and holding of the infant. As time passes and the child learns to talk, parenting increasingly should become the giving of psychological support and counsel and the teaching of children to do things, rather than your doing things for them.

Good parenting is not a matter of the number of hours you spend in the house with your children. You can spend the day at home doing housework and have no more communication with your children than to scream at them when they track mud into the house. Or you can stay home and spend several hours talking with them and be a good parent. Or you can be gone all day, flop in front of the TV when you get home and be a failure as a parent. Or you can be gone all day and spend your first hours home sharing with your children the highlights of the day and how you each felt about it and be a quality parent.

What do mothers have to gain from equal parenting? In the child's infancy, Mother will not have to bear the sleeplessness, physical labor, and isolation that contribute to many new mothers' postpartum blues. She will be less exhausted and will be able to continue being involved in the outside world at some level.

Mother will have outside interests so she will not have to get all her satisfactions from her children during their childhood. She will not have to feel that her status depends on how her children behave, so she will not have to pressure them. She can avoid the demonic role some mothers have fallen into of policing the feelings of everyone in the family. She will be free to do what is best for the child, not what she thinks a mother is supposed to do. She can be sure someone is home after school for the child to talk to if that is best. Or she can realize, as one mother did, that her child needed a few hours of playing to put a perspective on school problems; if she insisted on being with the child right away he would sob over minor slights and misunderstandings at school, but, given a cooling off period, the boy realized things were basically fine at school. Again, the mother will have her husband to share such decisions and the physical labor involved in child care.

During the children's adolescence, Mother will have kept up her own profession or outside interests so she will not have the nobody-needs-me or empty-nest syndrome. She will be able to loosen the reins on her children and finally let them go, proud that they are independent but still fulfilled by her own life, a feeling she will share with a father who is equally proud because he had just as much to do with the development of these independent, fully functioning adults.

CHAPTER 8
HOW TO RAISE NONSEXIST CHILDREN

Most parents want their children to get a better start in life than they did, and, for parents in an equal marriage, that will include helping the children to prepare to be equal partners in their own marriages or to be self-sufficient if they do not marry.

Fortunately, the very things that parents do to make their own relationship equal will be the things that help their children. Nothing teaches children how to behave as effectively as the modeling their parents do for them. From infancy your children are watching your behavior as individuals and using it as a standard by which to judge other people's behavior, but they are also watching your marriage to find out how marriage works and how marriage partners behave.

When they see you treat each other with respect and affection, the children will learn to expect respect and affection in their own marriages. When they see Father cook a meal and wash the family's dirty shirts as well as mow the lawn, they will see that men can freely participate in all kinds of household chores, and the boys will feel comfortable learning to be self-sufficient. When the children see Mother repair a leaky faucet and wash the car in addition to sewing ripped seams, they will see that women can do all kinds of chores, and the girls will be open to learning mechanical and outdoor skills. They will learn by example that there are no such things as masculine chores and feminine chores.

When your children listen to your conversations, they will find that both of you are capable of logic—as long as there is no resort to "you women are so illogical," which is merely a way of name-calling anyway. When they see both parents able to express joy, anger, sorrow, and pain without Father's feeling it unmanly to be emotional, they will learn to keep in touch with their own emotions. Children really do learn best by example.

Children begin being forced into sex roles in the hospital when they are born. Research has shown that blue is a more stimulating color for babies than pink, so wrapping boys in blue blankets and girls in pink starts them off at a different level of stimulation. Some nurses have also been found to respond differently to boy and girl babies: when the girls cry they rush to soothe them, but when the boys cry they tend to praise the boys' powerful lungs and loud voices as signs of great masculinity. If you can find a hospital that allows your baby to room with the mother and you to bring your own blankets, you may be able to escape having this early influence initiated without your consent.

Names have powerful effects on people. We know that a child given a name thought of as "creepy" in our society will be treated in ways that tend to mold the child into a "creep," although that isn't automatic and can be overcome. Still, we have not studied the effects of names on sex-role expectations, and it just may be that extremely "feminine" or "masculine" names might tend to push children toward extremes of sex-role stereotyping, so you might consider that before you name your boy Butch and your girl Marigold or whatever names are thought of in those terms in your culture.

Many behavioral scientists believe that parents, relatives, and other adults behave differently toward each sex from the very beginning and so help to shape the children's personalities into typical masculine or feminine behavior. It is said that we tend to cuddle and comfort girls from the start but roughhouse and tease boys. Try to give your baby both the security of cuddling and the adventure of roughhousing to avoid conditioning him or her stereotypically.

From the beginning you'll want to provide your child with all types of play and exploration experiences. Babies of both sexes usually get rattles and stuffed animals and mobiles. After that, they begin to be channeled. Girls get domestic toys—dolls, doll houses, furniture and clothes for dolls—craft sets, nurse kits, as well as some neutral toys like skates and games. Boys get transportation toys—trains, cars, boats, airplanes, and road-building equipment—sports equipment, guns, building toys, plastic model kits, doctor kits, monsters, and the neutral toys. Such toys begin programming boys to drive cars, become engineers, aspire to be doctors or mechanics or truck drivers or football players, and to be action-oriented. The girls' gifts program them to become wives and mothers and nurses and to be home-oriented.

Relatives and friends will give your children sex-typed toys. If you have a good relationship with your relatives, you could talk to them about their toy selection. If not, accept the toys they send and provide your child with the other-sex toys that are not being given. We aren't advocating a role reversal so that boys get only dolls and girls get only action toys. Toys are important for children to rehearse future roles. Both boys and girls need dolls to practice being parents. Both need cars to practice driving. Both need a wide variety of occupational toys to try future ways of earning a living. And both need building toys to teach them mechanical skills.

From almost the beginning, we tend to dress boys and girls differently. We put ruffled panties over the toddler girl's diaper because she looks so cute swinging her little bottom. We put the boy in practical overalls so his knees will be protected. We dress the girl in a fancy dress that mustn't be soiled or torn and that doesn't protect her. We warn her to keep her skirt down for modesty. We put the boy in pants that automatically protect his modesty and his body, and we chuckle "boys will be boys" when he comes in dirty with holes in his clothes. Even when girls wear pants, they often have no pockets, are not durable, and may not even be washable. Girls' jackets have less padding so they will "look attractive," while boys' are well padded so they can stay out in the cold longer.

Be sure your children of both sexes are dressed in sturdy clothes for play and that they are warm in winter and cool in summer, regardless of looks. In raising a nonsexist daughter, you'll want to think twice about her wearing a beautiful but unlivable dress for all but purely ceremonial occasions when another type of clothing would shock part of the family. With this concession, you'll want to explain to your child that she must wear this to Aunt Jane's wedding, but right afterward she may change into her comfortable clothing.

As your children begin to master the language, tell them what you believe. If you tell them it's OK for men to wash dishes and iron clothes and then they see their father doing it, they will be convinced. If you tell them one thing but live by another principle, they will become confused.

Teach your children your skills regardless of sex. Boys need to know how to cook and sew. Girls need to know how to fix things and do yard work. If you have a hobby, let your child try it. The more possibilities they are familiar with, the more your children will be able to choose interests that are right for them.

Expect your children to contribute to the family by doing whatever chores are possible at their own level. If you begin with a toddler's helping to pick up toys after play, running errands such as "take this to

Daddy," the child will always expect to be involved.

Children can do amazing things if they are allowed and encouraged to do as much as possible. Many preschoolers are able to fix their own breakfast if the dishes and cereal boxes are stored where they can be reached. Some primary-grade children can get up, eat, dress, and leave for school without assistance. Elementary-grade students can do a variety of cooking and baking, yard work, and house cleaning. From junior high, children can take responsibility for their own clothes and room, transport themselves by bus or bike, care for younger children, cook, and function at a near-adult level.

Children who learn to contribute as much as they can to the family and who gain such responsible skills will find it easier to be equal partners in a marriage when they are grown. They will not be afraid to do something traditionally done by the other sex, and they will know how to do all the things necessary for a comfortable life. They will also be prepared to survive in college, before marriage, and after a marriage ends. They will be healthier because they will have confidence in their own ability to cope.

Children benefit even in childhood from contributing to the family chores. They gain a feeling of self-worth that affirms them, and they gain a feeling of confidence that they can master increasingly difficult skills.

Parents, of course, benefit also because they will have fewer chores to do and more time for themselves, each other, and the family. Another way in which you will be teaching your children will be by the language you use. If you hear yourself talking about the fireman, postman, cameraman, newsman, or "every man has a right to expect . . ." when you mean all people, you may be giving your children the idea that only men can have those jobs or that only men have certain rights. Use the word *man* to mean male human being, and use more inclusive words when you aren't specifying sex—fire fighter, mail carrier, photographer or camera operator, journalist, and "everyone has a right." For years women have been told that the word *man* includes them, yet they have found themselves excluded from most of the man professions and men's rights and responsibilities.

Another common way of making women feel excluded is using *he* or *his* as a second reference, as in "The fire fighter is ready to give *his* life." It doesn't matter that the first reference included both sexes, since the second indicates only a man would hold the job. You can get around that by making the first reference plural so the second reference is *they* or *their.* Or you can use the second person, *you,* instead of third person in many instances.

Language really does affect as well as reflect our thinking, and it helps children to know that when you say *man* or *he* you clearly mean male and that in your speech you are including women as possible members of all professions and of all humanity.

As the children get older and begin to make tentative career choices, they will need your guidance and support if they choose nontraditional careers. Children need to know that there are many choices available to them, and they need not feel certain careers are impossible for them because of their sex. Girls especially need to know they can be mommies and still have outside careers since they will hear much propaganda to the contrary. But parents who are trying to raise children who are not sexual stereotypes will have to be careful not to force nontraditional roles on their children and not to recoil in horror when their daughter announces she wants to be a ballerina or their son says he wants to be a football player. In their early years children will try out several roles they will eventually discard, and, in a nonsexist society in which people are free to choose their professions according to interests and skills, both sexes will be represented in most professions. We will always have some female nurses and some male doctors, female dancers in the ballet, female teachers, and male police officers in addition to the members of the other sex who will join those professions. What we are aiming for is a wider choice for people, not a reversal of their old sex-role limitations.

Eventually your children will become teen-agers and will begin dating. That is when they will really need your support and counsel since they will be out of step with many teen-agers of the other sex. Not subscribing to sex roles, your daughter will expect to pay her share on dates and will feel free to ask boys out or call them up instead of moping around hoping the phone will ring. Your son will expect his dates to share the expense, open their own doors if their hands are free, and show him they are interested by calling him some of the time. They will need your sympathetic ear and your help in figuring out how to avoid compromising their principles while helping their dates to understand why they behave as they do and why they believe it is a better way to live.

Obviously, from toddlerhood on, home isn't the only place where children learn. They will be influenced by their peers, school, television and radio, books, and movies. You can't isolate them from such sources, and it wouldn't help them anyway. They would be cut off from all the good teaching these sources have to offer, and they wouldn't be prepared to face the sexist world when they grew up.

Innoculation is the best defense. Even in your own home the children are likely to hear that "men don't cry" and "wrestling isn't ladylike." You won't tell them that or any of the other stereotypes about men and women, but visitors may, or their playmates may, and the television dialogue probably will.

Go ahead and let your children watch television shows and commercials that stereotype women and men, but watch with them. Explain what is wrong with the assumptions being made or with the language being used. Talk back to the set if you feel like it. Put your nonsexist position squarely against the shows and advertisers. It will help your children understand your position, will arm them with the arguments they will need in the future, and will develop in them the healthy skepticism we all need to have about advertising especially but also about television programming generally.

If you are around when other children or adults make sexist remarks, you can later explain to your child what the other person's wrong assumption was. When you hear a boy call another little boy "a girl because you pull hair," you can explain later that pulling hair is not a characteristic of girls and women and that calling another boy a girl as an insult implied that the child regarded girls as inferior. You can also reframe much of what your child hears as being part of "the old belief."

When your child hears an interview on television in which someone claims that "women aren't strong enough to be fire fighters," you can explain that not all women are strong enough and not all men are strong enough, but only those who are physically capable will get the job. "People used to think that there were no women strong enough to be fire fighters, so they didn't allow women to take the test, but now we know that some women can pass the test, so they are becoming fire fighters," you can say.

The school system seems determined to divide the sexes against each other, so, as soon as your child is under the system's influence, you will have to counteract the institution's sexism, while not undermining its authority so much that your child believes nothing that is taught.

Schools have organized children in boys' lines and girls' lines for no educational reason but simply because they always have. Our son asks, "How come the girls' line always goes first to the library no matter how good we are or how bad they are?" Sexism—ladies first—is the answer.

Schools may pit boys against girls in sports and spelling bees, training them for a rivalry which will only impede their cooperating with each other in equal marriage and in a nonsexist work world. The children are divided according to sex for physical education from the beginning in many schools, even though the real differences in the physical skills of the sexes do not appear until puberty.

In the first grade, children learn about the family, and mother and father are put in the old stereotypical roles, even though 51 percent of school-age children have working mothers.

The textbooks your children will study frequently will tell stories that put down women or will use examples that are based on traditional sex roles.

Point out such violations to your child, and explain why they are wrong. Write notes to the teacher and principal, organize other parents, lobby the school board and legislature. But if you have innoculated your children, they will not be indoctrinated by sexism.

Instead they will be challenging the assumptions and statements that are based on stereotypes of the sexes which they hear at school. One eight-year-old was told that the class model-airplane-building project was for boys only. Being well innoculated, he challenged the rule in class, opened a class discussion about it, and was asked to prepare a speech on women's liberation. His teacher continued to make sexist remarks, but she began glancing at him each time and correcting herself. Our children themselves, being present in the classroom daily, can be the most potent force we have for ending sexism in the schools.

Even peer-group pressure can be resisted when a

child is innoculated. The same little boy, after the discussion on women's liberation, was the only boy in the class who voted with all the girls when the teacher asked "How many of you believe women should be equal with men?" He kept his hand up even after three other boys jumped him and tried to force his hand down. The other children teased him for a while, but he was sure of what he believed and they were not, and they eventually dropped the teasing and accepted him again.

You will know your children are innoculated when they are watching television in another room or playing outside with other children and they come in to report to you the "horrible sexist remark" they just heard. When that happens, you know they are not going to believe any of the propaganda for sexism they will be faced with. They will also be ready to correct you! Our son reminds us occasionally, "Even if he *is* a man, you should call him the milk deliverer."

You may wonder whether you want to experiment with your children, whether this has ever been tried before. We can assure you that our children, a grade-school boy and a high-school girl, are being raised this way. Our daughter has discovered that, far from discouraging boyfriends, her attitude of equality and her willingness to share the cost of a date attracts boys. After only a year of conscious training in a nonsexist attitude, our son's consciousness had also been raised; he was the eight-year-old mentioned above.

But nonsexist child-rearing was begun even longer ago than that. One of this book's authors, Jean, had parents who accidently raised her without sex-role stereotyping.

My mother describes her marriage as traditional, and she did not work outside because my father didn't want her to. I know my father was a traditionalist by the fact that he refused to let me wear pants until the cold weather in my first grade forced him to change his mind. Circumstances forced them to raise my brother and me as nonsexists, however.

We lived at the radio station where my father worked, so both parents stayed home. I had no idea that he was paid and she was not; they handled it as their joint money. My mother did all the heavy work to spare my father's weak heart. My father spent much of his time in the workshop of the radio station, and my mother did the cooking, but I assumed they made those choices by preferred interest, not by sex role, because they also had a policy of treating my brother and me with total impartiality. Whatever one of us got to do, so did the other. We lived in the country with no other children or adults nearby, so our parents entertained us by involving us in their work, or else we played together. At a very early age, our mother had us both learning to roll dough, mix cookies, and make gelatin. At the same age, our father taught us to use a drill press, soldering iron, and all the usual hand tools to keep us occupied in the workshop.

People, including our parents, gave us sex-typed toys, but we always played together and thought of the toys as both of ours. With our father always in the house and assuming a major share of child care, I could never have imagined a way to play house without a daddy and my brother was always ready to play the part. When it was time to play cowboys or to build highways, we split up his cowboy set so we each had part of a western outfit and shot it out with one gun and a cocked finger, or we shared the cars and road-building equipment, orchestrating fiery crashes with each other. Eventually our parents realized they *had* to buy my brother a doll and me a gun so we would be properly equipped for what we were already playing.

Going to school was a shock for me since that made me the only person in the house who had to leave every day. I found every excuse to stay home, and I soon found when I did go that they weren't telling the truth at that school. They explained how father went to work and mother stayed home. I knew that wasn't true. Later they showed us pictures of male doctors and said women could be nurses—our doctor was a woman, so I knew *that* wasn't true. They always showed the mail deliverer as a male, but our rural route was serviced by a woman sometimes. Of course I didn't believe what they said about firemen or policemen or much else—they hadn't passed my test of reality.

When I wanted to become a cowgirl—which I thought was a female doing the same work as a cowboy—and later a front-line soldier, my parents didn't laugh or try to dissuade me since they knew it would never happen anyway.

When my father died, my mother taught school, kept house perfectly, and had the best yard on the block. She was living proof that a woman could do everything normally expected of two parents, exhausting as that may have been.

Accidentally my parents had innoculated me. I went all through junior high and high school and most of college surrounded by sexism in school, in books, on television, and among my friends, but I didn't even see it. It wasn't until my second year of college, when I dated a man who was threatened by my getting higher grades and who kept telling me how a woman was supposed to behave, that I even realized anyone in the world discriminated against and stereotyped women. By that time, I could hold my own.

One of the biggest fears parents have of raising their children in a nonsexist way, they have told us frequently, is the fear that their children will become homosexuals. We can think of much worse things which could happen to a child, but we don't believe it works that way.

It hasn't happened in the cases of nonsexist child-rearing that we know of. In fact, it is our belief that the number of homosexuals will decrease if nonsexist child-rearing becomes common.

Most theories of people's becoming homosexual are framed in the context of a sexist society.

Freudians say homosexuality is caused by a weak or absent father and a strong mother. They tend to equate this with a role reversal, being raised themselves in a society which says women should be weak and men strong. But we believe the same facts just as clearly indicate that having a nonparticipating father contributes to homosexuality.

Lionel Ovessy, in the book *Sexual Inversion* edited by Judd Marmer, claims that homosexuality in a man is his reaction to dependency and power, developing in men at a time when they feel they are failures in the masculine role. The man, Ovessy says, represents himself in an equation: I am a failure as a man = I am castrated = I am a woman = I am homosexual.

We think that if men did not have to live up to an artificial sex role and were not taught to scorn women, they would not have to feel they were failures as men and would never make the equation, which depends on the idea that women are failed men.

Ovessy also suggests another aspect: homosexuals and lesbians have been taught to fear punishment for heterosexual contact and thus direct their sexuality to a safer object, a same-sex person. The strong presence of both sexes in the home, affirming their other-sex children's sexuality, could counteract this.

An acquaintance of ours says she traces the roots of her lesbianism to her parents' preference for her brother simply because he was a boy. She learned that being a boy was rewarded, and so she emulated him in everything, including being sexually attracted to women. If her parents had not been sexist, her life could have been different.

Lately a number of women have been turning to female lovers simply because there are no nonsexist men available to them. They want an equal relationship, but most of the men in their age range can understand only a male-dominated relationship. They find that with another woman, just as in an equal heterosexual marriage, the roles are not predetermined.

Parents who are unhappy about the sex of their child sometimes raise the child as though the boy were a girl or the girl were a boy. The child feels the other sex is preferred and tries to become one with the other sex. If both boys and girls were given the same toys and opportunities and had similar relationships with their parents as we are advocating, no one would have to treat a child of one sex differently from the other, and this confusion would not take place.

We have also talked with a transvestite who told us he "always wanted to wear lovely things, to express the feminine side" of his personality. But if boys weren't taught that they must repress their emotions and wear only utilitarian clothing, no men would become transvestites. They could express that part of themselves as men. In fact, most transvestites today are older men; the younger men who might have become such are fashion plates in their lace and satin shirts, rhinestone-studded pants, and platform shoes.

Forcing your children into rigid sex roles will not keep them from becoming homosexual. It will only make them into half-persons, unable to function fully in our society, unable to have an intimate marriage.

Giving your children a chance to explore all possibilities and ways of behaving will not make them become homosexual, and we think it could even prevent such a development.

Giving children a chance to learn many ways of behaving and many skills will not necessarily erase all differences between the sexes. Any *real* differences will show themselves naturally when we treat persons of both sexes the same way. We do not have to force people into artificially created roles to have them develop natural differences. In fact, if there are differences that are natural, there is no way that we could possibly keep them from showing up, no matter what education, customs, dress and hairstyles, or family patterns we adopted.

Treating boys and girls the same will give both sexes a chance to develop their full potential. As a society we need that full potential from every citizen. As parents we want that fulfillment for all our children.

CHAPTER 9
HOW TO GET TO EQUALITY FROM WHERE YOU ARE

Many couples want an equal marriage, or they think it sounds like a good idea, but they don't know how to get it. Wherever you are, whether you are just thinking about marriage or have been married many years in a traditional relationship or a near-equal one, you may find some solutions among the following suggestions to the questions of how to choose an equal partner, how to examine your own attitudes, how to establish the ground rules for an equal relationship, how to change your language, and how to negotiate change. If you already have an equal marriage you are used to breaking new ground and challenging accepted rules for marriage, so you probably will enjoy seeing some principles you can agree with which will affirm the way you are running your marriage.

If you have not chosen your marriage partner or are

dating someone but are not sure this is the right person—

it is important to choose the right partner, someone capable of having an equal relationship;

it is easier to have an equal marriage from the beginning than it is to start in the traditional sex roles and eventually evolve to equality;

it isn't impossible for a marriage to become equal, but, as long as you're just getting started, you might as well save yourself the time and effort involved in changing by starting with equality.

First, choose someone who agrees with you that an equal relationship is best, one who is willing to make a commitment to equality in principle, if not consistently in practice.

Marry someone who treats you with respect, kindness, and a minimum of game-playing. Unless your partner respects you, wants the best for you, and is not trying to out-psych you, you will have no basis for asking for equality.

By game-playing we mean patterns of behavior that are repeated over and over with the goal (often unconscious) of getting something out of the partner without having to ask for it in a straight way. Games include the well-worn "hard to get" and "if you loved me you would," both common in courtship. If you are open yourself, the other person usually will follow your lead, unless she or he is addicted to game-playing. So take the risk of being honest early in the relationship and avoid the pain of "romantic disillusionment" after you are married.

Marry someone who is flexible, who isn't afraid to

try something new or to change plans or learn something different. People who have equal marriages are pioneers in a new society, and they must not be afraid of forging their own rules and being a little different. In the old style of marriage, your roles were assigned to you by sex and never changed. In equal marriage, you will be changing assignments, rules, and behavior to be appropriate for each situation, so you cannot become complacent.

If you want children, marry someone who likes children and likes being involved with them, not someone who thinks they are cute or that one *ought* to have them. If you don't want children, marry someone who also plans to find fulfillment in other ways and who will be satisfied to enjoy other people's children occasionally. That doesn't mean that neither of you will change and develop a conflict later, but at least you start out together.

Marry your best friend—a person you like, respect, and trust. Don't expect to make major changes in your partner later. Some changes are possible, but you cannot know in advance whether your partner will change in the way you want. If you marry your best friend, you will be able to confide in each other freely and trust each other's motives.

Marry a person with whom you have much in common. That is true for any marriage, equal or not, but do get beyond the superficial. How do you feel about religion? Politics? Sex? How money should be spent? How time should be spent? What you want your life to have been like when you reach the end? Talking about such questions will establish whether you have similar philosophies of life. In an equal marriage, you need to agree as much as possible since you will be facing pressure from some parts of society for not conforming to sex-role stereotypes, and you won't want to be at odds with each other as well.

Make sure the person is right for you before you allow yourself to be swept away, to fall in love. While a "chemical attraction" is nice, it isn't love. Despite years of brainwashing by movies and television which have convinced many that love is simply a matter of looking at the right person and hearing bells, you actually *do* have control over whether you fall in love, or at least over whether you act on a purely physical attraction.

If you have found the right person or are already married, begin building your equal marriage by examining your own attitudes.

Examine your own unconscious assumptions about the behavior of men and women. How should it differ? Is there behavior you would approve of in a man but not in a woman or vice versa? What things that women customarily do would you be uncomfortable seeing a man do and vice versa? Why? Is there validity to your assumptions about the roles of the sexes, or were they simply passed on to you by our culture?

If you find that you can intellectually erase most of the differences in behavior of the sexes that you have been taught all your life, then you will be ready to change your behavior. A few people will claim that they can change their intellectual beliefs about the sexes, but they cannot change their emotional beliefs.

If you find that true, ignore your emotions and make some small but specific changes in your behavior based on your new intellectual outlook. Eventually, your emotions will follow. You will see that you have not turned into a member of the other sex or been scorned by society or whatever it was that you feared.

One couple began a discussion in which the wife, who had changed her name to the husband's but hated doing it, proposed that working women should be allowed to use their birth names in their careers while using their husbands' names at home. They got into a bitter argument, with tears on both sides. They continued the discussion over the next eight months and the husband gradually agreed intellectually but said he would feel ashamed if his wife did that. When she finished graduate school, she took her first job in her birth name, with his reluctant consent, as an experiment. At first he didn't want to admit to people that they used different names sometimes, and the wife took great care to drop off the cleaning, leave film to be developed, and order things using her married name, but eventually the two names began to overlap. Instead of being a social outcast, the husband found himself the object of a great deal of interest. People wanted to know why they did it, if it was legal, and how it worked. Some people were critical, but others expressed admiration and said they wished they had the courage to do it. Eventually the husband became totally committed to the idea of separate names, not just at work but socially as well, and he began introducing his wife with her own last name and proudly explaining the whys and hows to people who asked. His behavior preceded his emotional commitment, but eventually his emotions caught up with his mind.

If you are married, examine the way you and your spouse divide the responsibilities. Why did you divide them that way? Were any responsibilities assigned purely on the basis of sex? If they were assigned on the basis of skill, were you each skilled only in areas traditionally assigned to your sex?

Many couples just beginning to examine their attitudes about the sexes have noticed, for example, that when they go somewhere together, the husband automatically takes the driver's seat, and the wife just as automatically takes the passenger's seat. They sometimes discover they are doing it even when they are taking her car or when he is the one who is tired or has been driving all day. When they realize that they have assigned driving solely on the basis of sex, they decide on new rules, whether they will discuss it each time and decide on who most feels like driving or whether the person whose car they take will do the driving.

If you are not married, ask yourself the same questions about the roles you play with your dates, about your parents' marriage, and about any previous marriage you may have had. Are you falling into sex roles in your dating? Do you want to follow your parents' example? Did you play a sex role in a previous relationship?

If you are a woman, ask yourself what you would plan for your life if you did not have to consider a husband and possibly children. What kind of work would you do? Where would you live? What kinds of recreation or community activities would you participate in? Then ask yourself why you can't do those things and be married and maybe have children too. Of course, some jobs and recreations are so time-consuming or dangerous that people of either sex would have trouble holding them and being married or having families. And some places to live could endanger children's health and education. But rethink whether the family responsibilities that are holding you back really *have* to hold you back, given the cooperation of your partner in an equal marriage.

If you are a man, ask yourself what you would like to be doing with your life if you did not have to support or plan to support a wife and/or children. Would you change careers, go back to school, stay home for a while, move to a different place? If your wife shared the job of earning the living and you were under less pressure to take the job that paid most, could you have more of the things you really want out of life?

Whichever sex you are, think back to your childhood. How did being a girl/boy shape your life? What toys of the other sex would you have liked to own? What classes would you have liked to take? What skills do you wish you had that were only taught to the other sex? What activities did you participate in that you did not want to take part in but felt you had to because you were afraid of what people might think? How have you been discriminated against because of your sex?

By taking time to consider each one of these questions and others which occur as the result of your answers, you will have cleared up your own ideas of how the sexes are alike and different, have thought of some ways you would be happier if life were different, and have thought of some concrete suggestions for how you and your partner could create an equal marriage.

But wait—don't rush things. Have you told your spouse or future spouse about what you are thinking? Communication is the most important part of marriage, so don't leave it out here, in this important step toward changing your behavior. If you aren't talking about the changes in your own thinking, the behavior changes you are about to request will come as a shock for your spouse, who won't have had time to do the kind of preliminary thinking you have done. Besides, if you give your spouse a chance to share the thinking, your spouse may have some changes to request too, so you won't be the only one asking or realizing things could be better.

Tell your spouse how you answer each of the questions asked so far, what you have discovered about yourself, and how sex-role stereotyping has affected you. Begin at the beginning and you won't be dumping a huge load of discontent on your spouse all at once. You'll be more in harmony philosophically and closer emotionally if you do the sharing of your feelings, the changing of attitudes and discoveries about your own behavior and your marriage *before* you get around to asking for specific changes.

Women must be especially careful here and throughout the process of evolving an equal relationship not to use such women's liberation terms as *male chauvinist, male supremacist,* and *sexist pig.* Since these terms have become common, many women are tempted to use them because they are handy ways of saying you are being oppressed. Resist that temptation. Such terms are destructive to your relationship. They put a man squarely in the camp of the enemy; they separate him from you psychologically. In equal marriage, you want to be on the same team, helping and supporting each other, cheering each other on. That can't happen if you are in separate camps. You can explain to him how you are in a one-down position and how you want to be equal to him, and you will be saying the same thing without insulting him and without making him close his mind to any of your suggestions.

For both spouses, remember who your partner is and talk to him or her, not to "a member of the other sex." Some men are only dimly aware that women are the same species as they, and some are unable to treat either sex as human beings. Some women have that same inability to relate to other people. They need professional help with their human relationships. Other people have treated the other sex as equal all their lives, but they use the language that puts women down, even though their language is in conflict with their real understanding of people. All they need is to change their way of talking about the sexes.

Remembering who your partner is can be useful in helping your partner change. You can help your partner see that sex-role stereotyping and its traditional division of behavior and duties is unfair; and most people in our culture—especially sports fans—value fairness so highly that they will be appalled at the idea that they could have been unfair.

A person interested in civil rights, history, or patriotism can understand that equality of the sexes is extending the American dream which was first a search for freedom of religion, then came to include other freedoms for white property-owning males, then was extended to nonpropertied men, then to men of other races, and is now being taken a step further to include women.

A religious person can see that we are all God's children and should treat one another as such.

Give your spouse a chance to change. You didn't arrive at your conclusions about sex roles instantly, and your spouse won't either. It is hard to resist pointing out that your spouse's statement today is just what you said last week, but you must resist. The fact that your partner has adopted your argument means she or he has accepted it. To point out the change simply means an argument about what each of you really said last week instead of using that energy to move ahead. Forget it and keep your eye on the main goal—sharing your changing attitudes and beliefs in preparation for changes you will want to make in your marriage.

Try to discuss sex roles and your thoughts about them when you have privacy and when you are not angry so you can be completely honest with each other. If you are angry, discuss what you are angry about, but don't get off the subject into a general discussion of sex-role stereotypes. You will find that discussions with friends and watching movies and television commercials will spark further discussions between you. If you know some people who have equal marriages, it also helps to socialize with them so that you both can see equal marriage in action and feel less alone.

Again, the most important thing you can do is keep the lines of communication open between you.

Once you have examined your own attitudes and shared with your partner, learn and use the language of equality.

Don't let your language reflect unconscious assumptions about people on the basis of sex. Be aware of what you are saying.

Don't call women girls. By now you realize that it denies them their adulthood.

Drop all those folksy sayings about the sexes: act like a man; boys will be boys; woman's place is in the home; behind every great man is a woman; the hand that rocks the cradle rules the world; it's a man's world. Don't use phrases like "woman driver" or "Isn't that just like a man?" or "pushy woman" or "male chauvinist" even as a joke. Once you are comfortable living in an equal marriage, you can make such jokes because your spouse will know you aren't serious, but at first you need to be superconscious of the language. Even when you later feel comfortable making such jokes, make them in private since other people might think you are serious, especially children, for whom you want to set a good example.

Think about what you are saying. If you call a wife "the better half," "the ball and chain," or "the old lady," what are you saying about the relationship? Why do you say "woman author" and "male nurse"—because you expect authors to be men and nurses to be female?

Avoid using *man* for humankind and words which end in *-man,* because they leave women out. Make your examples plural so you won't have to use *he* as a second reference.

Language may not seem to be one of the most important things to take care of. By now you may be eager to get on with deciding who will do the dishes. But language is important, too, since it not only reflects our thinking but shapes it as well. As you change your language, you will rid your mind of unconscious assumptions, stereotypes, and prejudices. You will be free to work on your equal relationship without having to fight the old biases.

Now you are ready to negotiate changes in behavior.

You will want to establish the ground rules for an equal marriage: equal responsibility for chores, children, sex, earning a living, and all other duties; joint decision-making and responsibility for handling money; tasks to be assigned on an individual basis, not on the basis of sex; and joint responsibility for the health of the marriage, communication between you the spouses, and your own continued growth.

That is quite a bit to tackle at once, so don't try. If you are not yet married it will be easier because you don't have to break old habits. Talk over each aspect of your future life and decide how you will handle it, realizing, of course, that you are free to make changes later when you actually begin living in your equal marriage.

If you have yet to be married, be sure to write your own marriage vows, the "constitution" of your marriage. You will work out the bylaws later as you live your marriage. You will want to promise each other a long-term commitment and promise each other that no other person will become central to your life in the way your spouse is. You will want to pledge yourselves to joint responsibility for all aspects of your life and for the health of your marriage. You will want to make other promises to each other which reflect your own values and goals for your life together. And you will want to specifically ask the minister not to use sexist language, such as pronouncing you "man and wife"—make it "husband and wife"—or saying "what God has joined together let no man put asunder"—make it "let no one put asunder."

If you are already married, you will have to break old patterns while developing new ones. For that reason, it may take longer. In fact, the first change will be the hardest. After that, you may move faster. Begin by asking yourself what is bothering you most about your present relationship. Make it concrete and specific. Once you know what change you want, sit down with your partner when you both have plenty of time and negotiate a change.

If a wife is most bothered by having to cook dinner and then clean up afterward every night, she can propose that the partners switch, each cooking one night and cleaning the next.

The husband may make a counterproposal that the wife do all the cooking and that he do all the cleaning or that they alternate by weeks or that they both cook and clean together. He might even reject an equal division but agree to give the wife a "vacation" one night a week.

In reaching your goal, bargain for the most significant change you can get, but take any change at all, no matter how small, rather than leave things as they are.

The husband, too, may want a change. If he is tired of working overtime to bring home enough money, he may propose that the wife get a part-time job so that he will have more time at home. They can trade the changes they want to make. But the decision isn't final and never is. A creative marriage means constantly trying new ways of doing things, searching for better ways.

When contracts need to be made or renegotiated or whenever you need straight communication with each other, here are some guidelines to follow. These do not add to or totally summarize the many good books written on straight communication and fair-fight techniques, but they do cover the essential points:

1. Keep your real goal in mind. If you aren't sure what you want, you will not be able to tell your spouse. Do not be sidetracked by trying to come out the winner or the "nice guy."

2. State your opinion and your feelings boldly with "I" statements. Be willing to say what you want as though you had the right—in an equal marriage you *do* have the right.

3. Listen to the feelings and opinions of your spouse. You like to be heard, to have your spouse really understand and appreciate what you say and feel, and so does your spouse.

4. Keep your goal in mind. Do not be sidetracked into a debate on a secondary matter such as who is in the right or who "always" wins the argument.

5. Know the difference between opinions and thoughts, which are subject to challenge, and feelings, which should not be. You both have the right to any feeling you happen to have. Your opinions or ideas may be wrong, but your feelings aren't.

6. Know the difference between *having* feelings, on the one hand, and, on the other, being "made" to react certain ways because you have those feelings. Actually, every time we have a feeling it is healthy for us to express it, and it is unhealthy for us to repress or deny it. But no behavior automatically follows from any feeling. You have available a wide variety of behavioral responses which would express a particular feeling, and you choose the one that seems best. For example, your spouse may do something which hurts you—makes you feel left out, rejected, or unrespected—and you may be tempted to respond with anger. But there are other responses available, and you do not have to choose a fit of temper. One of the more productive responses would be to keep your goal in mind and not be sidetracked into an expression of anger which will usually set up your spouse for another nonproductive exchange of angry words. A simple statement explaining that you feel left

out and rejected will usually commend your feelings to a loving spouse.

7. Own your thoughts, feelings, desires, and let your spouse own hers or his. Do not try to be a "we" until you have worked through your positions and clearly understand that what you are saying is definitely the position of your spouse, too.

8. Do not read your spouse's mind or expect your spouse to read yours. Occasionally your guess will be exactly right, to your surprise and delight, but don't make it a habit. It tends to limit your freedom and spontaneity. Say what is on your mind and ask your spouse to do likewise. Take the risk. Your spouse may disagree with you but will respect you for being straight and open.

9. Do not agree to any rules or accept any responsibilities that you don't intend to keep or that violate your integrity. Say yes only when you mean yes. It is better to disappoint your spouse when you say no than to disappoint your spouse and create future mistrust by saying yes when you don't really mean it and cannot or will not live up to it.

10. Keep your goal in mind. Do not be sidetracked by misunderstandings or hurt feelings. Persist. Be responsible for getting your own position presented and heard. Do not expect the other person to be protective or to baby you.

11. If you want to get your way, appeal to the other person's goodwill, sense of fairness, and commitment to the relationship. Do not resort to an appeal to your own righteousness or your own final authority. In an equal relationship, there *is* no final authority.

12. Avoid attacking or fighting back. A good relationship is not built on the sand of having "gotten in a good blow" but on the rock of patience, fairness, and persistence.

13. Avoid bringing in past issues, hurts, or injustices. Let the past be the past, except that we may have learned a little by having lived it. The only function past grievances have is that they keep the present issue from being resolved satisfactorily.

14. Be willing to settle for small or partial gains. Next week or next year you may be able to get a better contract or agreement if this one still is not livable.

15. Encourage those changes you like, however small they may be. You will find your spouse likes to please you when you let her or him know that you are pleased. It needn't be elaborate—a nice "thank you, I like that" will usually do.

16. Finally and most importantly, keep your goal before you. Your goal is to have a marriage that is more satisfying because there are two equals working together.

At first, negotiating small changes may seem too slow for you, but a couple who are good friends of ours are a good example of what can happen. She spent many years at home while he worked at a good job, but she wanted to go back to teaching in high school. He didn't want her to but agreed to it on the condition that nothing change at home: that she keep house, fix meals, and keep the clothes clean just as she always had. He rationalized that since they didn't need the money, her working was just a hobby and shouldn't detract from her *real* work of keeping house.

She agreed to his terms, except she got one small concession from him. On the evening when she did the major housecleaning chores after work, he would wash the dishes. Soon he was also fixing dinner that evening. Not long after that, he realized that she was spending all her time at home doing housework, so he began to pitch in so they could be together more. Even stranger for him, he discovered that he *liked* cooking and even enjoyed housework. A few years later he retired, well ahead of his wife, and became a full-fledged househusband. He is now famous in his neighborhood for his home-baked breads. Now that his wife has recently retired, it will be interesting to see how she negotiates to get some of the home chores back.

Undoubtedly, this couple followed rules of good communication, and the wife was especially careful to reinforce small changes in the right direction.

In Baja California, Mexico, ranchers used to have a hard time getting certain steers to go back to the ranch with the rest of the herd. Those steers which were unmanageable were tied to a burro and left out in the rugged country while the herders took the other steers to the ranch headquarters. Eventually, even though the steer was much stronger and heavier than the burro, the two would arrive back at the ranch. That happened because the burro would cooperate with the steer when it was headed in the direction of the ranch. When it would walk away from the ranch the burro would let itself be a dead weight. The burro reinforced the steer for every step it made in the homeward direction, and eventually they made it to the burro's goal, the ranch.

That story is meant to illustrate that persistence and patient rewarding of small steps in the right direction pay off. Don't criticize your spouse for the smallness of the change. Reward your spouse for having made any change at all. Eventually, you can reach your goal.

Of course, coming to an equal marriage isn't a straight linear process of choosing the right mate, getting your own attitudes changed, sharing with your partner, changing your language, and negotiating change. As you become more aware of how sex roles have affected you, you will discover more about sex-role stereotyping. And as you are making changes in your behavior, you will discover more language that needs changing and other facets of sex-role stereotyping.

All the steps will work together and will reinforce one another.

CHAPTER 10
INTIMACY: THE REWARD OF EQUAL MARRIAGE

The world is a lonely place. People work together, play together, talk together, but they are isolated from one another's true thoughts and feelings.

Most people keep their guard up, trying to avoid letting others find out what they truly are. In most situations, we hide behind facades of what we hope other people will think of us. If they try to get around the facade we become defensive and ward them off with rationalizations and games.

Only rarely can two people drop their facades and share their thoughts and feelings with each other without playing games. Most commonly that happens in a good marriage.

Intimacy is a two-way relationship in which the partners know each other as they really are, shortcomings and all, and yet they have no fear and do not have to play games with each other because they each are accepted genuinely by the other as a person with good times and bad, highs and lows. Intimacy is having no place to hide from your partner emotionally, yet not having any need to hide. It is a warmly personal being together characterized by self-disclosure and affection, as opposed to impersonal side-by-side relationships which take place in most settings. Intimacy is the experience of close, sustained familiarity with another person's inner life.

In intimacy there is no longer any need to play games because the purpose of games is to get your own way without having to accept responsibility for having wanted to get your own way. In intimacy each partner has the right to ask to get wants and needs met, and so the partners can avoid the noncreative way of asking—game-playing—and ask straight. Game-playing, as we have previously said, is the attempt to control another person without seeming to do so, and it is motivated by the fear that the other person is out to control you. Like a card game, each player must play cards "close to the chest" to avoid tipping off the other person. That is the opposite of intimacy in which you both lay your cards on the table.

Intimate partners don't read each other's minds. They really listen to each other, and they talk openly with each other so that they *do* eventually know each other's minds. Even though they do know each other, an intimate partner never assumes he or she can predict what the other will say or do; each leaves room to be surprised by the partner, for the partner to have grown in a way not expected.

Intimacy is the product of an equal-partnership

marriage. Equal marriages are not always intimate, but intimate marriages are always equal.

Intimacy demands respect and trust, and you cannot respect or trust an inferior enough to share your innermost secrets. A person who is in the one-down position in a relationship is at the mercy of the other person and so is almost forced to play games. Such a person is likely to try to convince the powerful partner that "if you loved me you would let me have my way." The issue then becomes whether the weak partner is loved, not whether what the weak partner wants is reasonable. The one-down person, having no power, may find that sex or praise or anything else the strong partner wants can be withheld until the strong partner gives in. The games do succeed in gaining a hollow victory for the weak person fairly often, but the games destroy trust and respect and a chance for intimacy.

In intimacy the partners must be free to be who they really are, even if society would not approve of that. In marriages that try to conform to sex-role stereotypes, the partners constantly must keep an eye on the stereotype and ask "How am I doing?" They cannot keep their focus on creating their lives as long as they have to keep checking their performance. Intimacy accepts a person completely regardless of outside standards. Intimates never have to force themselves into artificial molds. Only an equal marriage can give partners that freedom.

In an equal marriage, each partner can cope with the whole of married life, from household chores to breadwinning to getting the car fixed to caring for the children. Neither partner will panic for economic, social, or domestic reasons at the idea of losing the partner. Each will know that the other partner is there primarily for the emotional value of the relationship. That will free the partners to keep the emotional relationship close and healthy—intimate.

Intimates are committed to each other out of liking each other, not out of a feeling that although marriage may be a bad deal, getting out of marriage is worse. They are sexually faithful, not out of fear of getting caught, but out of the knowledge that keeping physical as well as emotional intimacy for the partner will strengthen the bond and also because they know that a committed sexual relationship is far greater than the superficial thrills of outside love affairs. Equal partners know there can be no double standard for fidelity; straying by either partner can hurt the marriage.

There are a few things that intimacy is not. It is not just saying anything that occurs to you, a stream of consciousness. Intimates give each other a measured honesty. They accept accountability for what their emotions will do to a spouse. Very negative thoughts about the spouse which might appear fleetingly are better left unsaid—Why compare your spouse's figure with someone you see on the beach when the difference is genetic? Since your spouse can't send back this body in exchange for a new one, sharing that thought can only hurt your partner. And if you should think your partner is having lustful thoughts about someone who might look better in a bathing suit than you think you do, it is better not to challenge your spouse on the spot—it is sometimes more constructive to leave your spouse some private thoughts. Intimacy is revealing to your spouse the sum total of where you stand, rather than revealing every small emotion which flits through you.

Novelist Leo Tolstoy was so much in love with his future wife that before they married he could not bear to have any secrets from her, so he gave her all his diaries to read. She could never forget or completely forgive him for the "wicked" life he had previously led. Later each of them kept a diary and let the other read it, no matter how negative the entries were toward the spouse. Eventually the marriage was destroyed by this unmeasured honesty.

Intimacy is not sameness. Intimate partners can accept each other as they really are. They don't have to pretend to like exactly the same things or be skilled at the same things or behave the same way. They can tolerate differences. In fact, they often can celebrate the differences which make each partner see things a little differently and let each partner look through two pairs of eyes by sharing.

Intimacy is not constant togetherness. Part of intimacy is being able to give your partner time and space to be alone when your partner wants privacy. Intimacy is responsible use of time—that is, not taking time away from the family, which is vital to its functioning and to the closeness of the partners. Each equal partner is accountable for how time is used. Your partner should know where you are and how long you will be there most of the time, but that does not mean asking permission. Each of you has the right to decide how to spend your time, but if you want intimacy that will have to include the choice to do your share of the chores and spend much of your leisure time with each other.

Intimacy is not total self-giving. In an equal marriage, each of you basically has two rights: the right to ask for what you want, as well as what you need, and the right to say no to anything your partner asks for if it violates your integrity.

Because each partner has those rights, no one has to play games to get a request granted. Each can ask straight and expect a straight answer. When something one partner wants conflicts with what the other partner wants, the two can compromise and find another alternative. No one will have to feel put-upon. Too much self-sacrifice can destroy intimacy as easily as self-centeredness can. Both partners must be happy with what they are getting out of the relationship for it to thrive.

Intimacy.is not without risks. Each spouse must trust that the other will not crush feelings that are revealed to the partner, but that may happen from time to time. The partner may not realize that this is a tender point or may use something shared in friendship against the partner during an argument. But each partner must also trust his or her own ability to recover if occasionally the spouse is careless with the revealed self. When you point out to your partner in an intimate marriage that your trust has been violated, partner usually feels worse about it than you do.

In intimacy, you may lose your pride. To reveal your inner self to your partner you will have to face yourself, and you will know that somebody knows the whole truth about you and loves you anyway. You may come to replace pride with a sense of humor about yourself. And, in fact, you could finally come to be able to live a day at a time without having to prove yourself to anyone, even yourself.

You could have an equal relationship with your spouse, develop an intimate marriage, and invest much of your time and your emotional energy in your spouse, and then lose your spouse by death. In fact, that will almost surely happen if you have an intimate marriage, because it isn't likely to end in divorce. That happened to both of us, and it was terribly painful. If you have an intimate relationship with someone, losing that person leaves a gaping hole in your existence. You feel as though most of you had died. But you will survive better for having had an equal marriage. You will know how to cope with every aspect of daily life which continues to need care, and you will survive physically. Having had an intimate relationship with your spouse, you will not feel guilty about things you later guess your spouse might have wanted; you will know that your spouse asked for everything he or she wanted and that you tried to give it if possible but that you always had an authentic relationship. Even a sick or dying person wants to be an equal, to know you are not pitying them or sacrificing yourself with one eye on what your friends will think. If you have an intimate marriage and your spouse faces a slow death, you will share your grief and comfort each other. And after your spouse dies, knowing what a precious thing an intimate marriage is and having had the experience of establishing one, you will be able to start again, knowing even better what you want and how to avoid some of the mistakes you may have made the first time.

If you decide for an equal and intimate marriage you will be forced to grow, and that can be painful. It is sometimes hard to give up the cheap ways you have developed to get what you want and to learn to ask straight. In order to ask for what you want, you will have to examine yourself and decide what it is that you really want out of life. You will have to learn to accept yourself and your partner as a gift, to know that you have done nothing to deserve this relationship and that you can do nothing to deserve it. You will be loved for what you are. If you are used to the feeling of being driven, of being under pressure to perform, you may have to give that up and accept being accepted.

An equal, intimate marriage will not lead to loss of freedom and stifling of growth but to different freedoms and a new potential for growth. Launching out in new directions might seem frightening with unknown consequences, unfamiliar territory, and no one to guide you. But with an equal partner you can dare much more, knowing you have the support and companionship of your partner and a place to come back to for sharing either your triumphs or your defeats.

EPILOGUE
KEEPING YOUR NAME— *A* SYMBOL OF EQUALITY

After we give a speech on equal marriage, the first question asked is usually "Why do you have different last names?"

Most commonly, people guess that we aren't really married or that we don't love each other very much, or they dismiss it as a nit-picking distraction from the real issues of equality for women.

Using separate names does not indicate that a couple is not married. Most states have no law requiring a woman to change her name at marriage. "How did you sign your marriage certificate?" many people ask. The answer is: the same way that most couples sign, using our own names. Likewise, having the same name does not indicate that a couple is legally married. Many a woman who is not married but lives with a man uses the man's last name to avoid letting people know they are not married.

If changing your name proved your love for your

partner, then American women love their husbands, while American men don't love their wives. On the other hand, it would mean that Egyptian, Chinese, and Icelandic couples do not love each other at all since their tradition is for the women to keep their own names. Russian women are given a choice, so the returns would be mixed. And Spanish-speaking women keep their own names but add de Garcia or whatever the husband's name is at the end—meaning their love is only an afterthought tacked on at the end? Of course not. Changing the name is only a matter of tradition, not an act of love.

As we have said, language shapes thought as well as being shaped by it. A woman's taking her husband's name—especially if she allows herself to be called Mrs. John Brown instead of using her own given name—implies that she is the secondary part of the marriage. A couple in which the wife takes the husband's last name can have an equal relationship. The world, however, will tend to see theirs as a male-dominant marriage.

That is because our custom of the woman's changing her last name originates from English common law. The law, according to Blackstone, stated, "By marriage, the husband and wife are one person in law; that is, the very being or legal existence of the woman is suspended during the marriage, or at least is incorporated and consolidated into that of the husband; under whose wing, protection, and cover she does everything." As the U. S. Supreme Court put it, the common law has in reality meant the husband and wife are one person" and that one is the husband."

In changing her name, the wife ceased to exist as an independent person in the eyes of the law and the community. So it is not trivial for women to want to keep their own names, for a person's independent existence is not trivial.

When the congregation rushes up to greet the new bride at the end of the wedding ceremony, many will call her by her husband's last name. By doing so they are reminding her of society's expectations for husband and wife—an unequal relationship with the wife in the one-down position.

For some women that is an exciting moment, a moment looked forward to from childhood, a symbol of womanhood. For many other women it is an uncomfortable moment, one in which they feel a loss of identity.

A name is very close to the core of our being. Our first name is one of the first words we learn, and we learn our family name while we are still quite small. To lose our name is to lose our sense of self. One newly married woman who had moved to a new apartment was asked to sign her name, address, and telephone number to return a wedding present and was surprised at herself when she burst into tears because "I can't even remember my name, address, or telephone number—I don't know who I am!"

When a woman changes her name, she cuts herself off from much of her past. Many friends will not know or remember her new name, so they will not be able to contact her. When she achieves something, while using her husband's last name, few old acquaintances will know of her accomplishment. If she is working at the time of her marriage, she will lose contact with former co-workers, bosses, clients, and contacts who might have been able to help her if they had known her name.

From a practical point of view, thousands of dollars could be saved every year if women did not change their names by marriage. When a woman changes her name, scores of work hours must go into notifying records keepers of the change and making the change. Such changes include social security, insurance policies, savings and checking accounts, driver's license, employment records, automobile title, credit cards, membership records for organizations, records of stocks and bonds purchased, passport, voter registration, and others. And frequently these must all be changed again if and when a woman remarries.

In fact, a Tennessee court recently suggested that the time may come when the law will require that all women keep their birth names unless they go to court to have them changed. The court cited as reasons endless paperwork and the difficulty in keeping track of women, whether it be for credit records or criminal records or to know the correct name of a woman for purposes of suing her.

Actually, the idea of a woman's keeping her birth name is not brand-new. The first person to keep her own name after marriage was feminist Lucy Stone who married Henry Blackwell in 1855. Before the marriage ceremony Henry read their protest against the laws which at that time made marriage virtual slavery for a woman, laws that included the husband's having custody over the wife's person, exclusive control of their children, ownership of the wife's personal property, and use of her real estate in most cases, and the right to any money earned by the wife.

Even then, Lucy Stone and Henry Blackwell said, "Marriage should be an equal and permanent partnership, and so recognized by law . . . until it is so recognized, married partners should provide against the radical injustice of present laws, by every means in their power."

Today the worst injustices have been corrected, but many laws and judicial decisions are still based on the idea of marriage as an unequal partnership. Equal partners today must still live their equality in the face of inequalities of the law, not in conformity to such laws.

In most states, it is perfectly legal for a woman to keep her birth name. All she has to do is leave all her records and documents in her birth name after she marries, fill out any new forms in her birth name, inform her friends and acquaintances and live for a while correcting people until her name is accepted as still her name. In some states she may even have to go to court to have her name legally "changed" back to her birth name.

People are usually curious to know what a couple will name the children if the parents are using different last names. Each couple will answer that differently. Some will name the child with the father's name, feeling it is obvious who the mother is, and thus naming the child acknowledges who the father is. Some might give a boy the father's name and a girl the mother's name. Some may prefer to make up a new name either out of parts of the parents names or a name unrelated to the parents' names. Most commonly, the child is given both parents' names, with or without a hyphen. Lucy Stone and Henry Blackwell had Alice Stone Blackwell, who grew up to carry on her parents' leadership of the feminist movement. Journalist Heywood Broun and feminist Ruth Hale had future sports commentator Heywood Hale Broun.

What happens when the children with double names get married and have children? We don't really know; that's up to them to decide. Probably they will have some choosing to do, but we hope it will be done on a better basis than automatically taking the father's father's name. At least they will realize that they are as much their grandmother's descendants as their grandfather's, as much their maternal grandfather's as their paternal grandfather's, and they will take pride in all the names that make up their heritage.

We've also been asked how our children feel about our having different names. When we married, they were old enough to realize Jean's keeping her birth name was something different and to wonder why. Once it was explained to them, however, they became very enthusiastic over—in fact, proud of—the fact. They don't mind being a little different from other people, and when they introduce us to their friends, instead of taking the easy way out—"Mom and Dad, this is Tommy"—they go out of their way to say "This is my dad, Richard Bright, and this is my mom, Jean Stapleton."

Finally, people worry whether Richard's ego is

battered because his wife keeps her own name. Richard says:

I always liked the romantic idea of the whole family having the same name so people would know you are a unit, but I thought about what it would be like if I had to change my name to make that possible. I have quite an emotional investment in my name. I've used it for many years, and I like it. All my friends and associates know me by it. I would feel lost if I changed it. And I realized that that is the way Jean would feel if she changed her name. If I wouldn't want to do that to myself, how could I do it to the person I love? Occasionally I do get hooked into assuring people that we really are married and explaining to them why Jean has kept her own name, but it's no big deal.

Actually, the whole idea of explaining why we keep our own names seems backward. When Jean was teaching third grade in a small town in New Mexico just before her first marriage, her students were amazed that she would be changing her name. Most of the eight-year-olds had assumed that their mothers were born with the same last name as their fathers. They wanted to know why the name change happened. Jean recalls:

I told them it was so everyone would know that the partners were married to each other and so the children would have one last name. Then we went around the room figuring out what each girl's name would be if she married one of the boys there. After school I met the fifth-grade teacher who gave me a ride to the city and told her how amusing my students had been—how I had had to explain to them why women changed their names at marriage.

The teacher responded, "I wish someone would tell *me* why."

I had 150 miles to think that over, and I couldn't think of a reason, satisfactory to an adult, why a woman should give up her identity.

We never have been able to find a good reason for changing. We have found a *logical* reason: it declares to all that this woman now belongs to this man, that she lives with him and cares for him and entrusts her future in his hands. Since the man is not changing his name to indicate the same things, there is an unequal relationship being created.

Since we are for equality, we don't think the logical reason is a *good* reason. We know some couples can have an equal marriage even though the wife takes the husband's last name, but we believe it adds an unnecessary burden to their struggle for equality.

SUGGESTIONS FOR FURTHER READING

The following short list of books has been selected for: (1) their general agreement with the thought of this book, and (2) their relatively nonsexist approach and language. Many books could be listed which are worth reading for their insight and style but which perpetuate the cultural sexist language and/or assumptions. In the mushrooming field of books on the feminist movement, there are many good, nonsexist books, but we have chosen to suggest only Gornick for a beginning "reader" in feminist literature.

Bach, George R., and Goldberg, Herb. *Creative Aggression: The Art of Assertive Living*. New York: Avon Books, 1975.

This excellent book on interpersonal relations exposes the secret tyranny of the "nice" guy, argues cogently the case for recognizing and accepting responsibility for our hostilities, and helps us to apply techniques for hostility expression and to creatively get what we need and want in interpersonal relationships.

Bach, George R., and Wyden, Peter. *The Intimate Enemy: How to Fight Fair in Love and Marriage.* New York: Avon Books, 1970.

Breaking with the tradition that suggests that fighting between intimates is something to avoid, Bach and Wyden show the necessity of conflict between intimates and teach how to make fighting a process whereby nobody loses, the relationship is strengthened, and real fairness prevails.

Bach, George R., and Deutsch, Ronald M. *Pairing.* New York: Avon Books, 1975.

Aimed at partners or partners-to-be, this is an excellent guide to achieving a more open, honest, and responsible intimacy.

Belliveau, Fred, and Richter, Lin. *Understanding Human Sexual Inadequacy.* New York: Bantam Books, 1970.

This is a very readable presentation of the basics of Masters and Johnson with a foreword by them. If you have had some difficulty wading through the original work of Masters and Johnson this is the book to read.

Deutsch, Ronald M. *The Key to Feminine Response in Marriage.* New York: Random House, 1968.

We suggest this book mainly for Chapter 6, which deals with the importance of the pubococcygeus muscle in sexual function or dysfunction.

Gordon, Thomas. *Parent Effectiveness Training: The Tested New Way to Raise Responsible Children.*

New York: Peter H. Wyden, Inc., 1970. (Also now available in paperback.)

This book is so good that you will not see how you got along with anyone before you read it. The approach Gordon takes is so obviously creative and fruitful that it is hard to believe we have not always parented in this way—but we haven't! This book is about listening, understanding, speaking in a straight (game-free) way, and owning our problems while we let others do the same. It is far more than a guide to parenting, however, as all its basic insights are applicable to *all* our relationships.

Gornick, Vivian, and Moran, Barbard K., eds. *Woman in Sexist Society: Studies in Power and Powerlessness.* New York: Basic Books, 1971.

This book is crammed with articles by thirty-one female activists and scholars. It is intended for those who want to get a feel for the women's liberation movement, to see what its concerns are, to have their consciousness raised. In separate sections the stereotypes of beauty and personality, woman's "nature," and political and employment arenas are challenged. A final section deals with feminist concerns in the fields of education, homosexuality, race, and radicalism.

Lederer, William J., and Jackson, Don D. *The Mirages of Marriage.* New York: W. W. Norton & Co., 1968.

This is a sound and scholarly work which lists seven false assumptions (myths) about marriage and attempts to rectify their destructive effects. It shows the systems concept of marriage, details destructive elements, offers ways to help yourself in your marriage, as well as advises when and how to get professional help.

Oden, Thomas C. *Game Free: A Guide to the Meaning of Intimacy*. New York: Harper & Row, 1974.

The subtitle of this book is a good description of it. After some tentative definitions of intimacy, Oden challenges the implicit faith of transactional analysis and argues the case for a deeper, more "realistic interpersonalism." What we call the intimacy of equals is akin to the kind of intimacy he calls for.

Stacy, Judith, Bereaud, Susan, and Daniels, Joan, eds. *And Jill Came Tumbling After: Sexism in American Education*. New York: Dell Books, 1974.

The editors have given us a fascinating array of articles documenting the *continuing* sex-role indoctrination which has been and is going on in our educational system. Article after article uncovers the obvious implanting of sex-role stereotyping in almost every phase of the education of our children. This is a worthy guide to parents who want to be aware of what they will have to begin to change in order to raise nonsexist children.